FEDERAL PLEA AGREEMENTS

A Soul to Keep

daniel storm

Books by: daniel storm

Reaper's Gate

Jury Duty

Praetorian Guard

Surviving the Alphabet Soup

The Apostle

Mantis

The Prey

Not Afraid to Kill, Not Afraid to Die

Masters of the Race

Watch for these titles in Spanish*

Federal Plea Agreements
by
daniel storm

Copyright 2014

ALL RIGHTS RESERVED BY THE AUTHOR. No part of this book may be reproduced or transmitted in any form or by any means, electronic or mechanical, including photocopying, recording, or by any information storage and retrieval system, and no copies, duplications or use of the following is permitted without the express, written consent of:

This book is a work of creativity, observation, research and experience. If any names, events and characters have any resemblance or similarities to actual persons, names, places or events in this story, it is purely coincidental, or the personal knowledge of the author.

ISBN #9780989974448

FEDERAL PLEA AGREEMENTS

Preface

As an author, I create both, informative and entertaining books for the general public. Quite often, I am asked where the ideas originated from or do I glean my novels from my experiences with the justice system. This book is a little different and I feel compelled to explain to all of you, the genesis for this travel guide to a frightening destination for anyone, along with the motivation.

I dedicate this book to a man who has taught criminal law for almost four decades and when I began my career, was my mentor and spiritual advisor for all things legal. **Walter Wolf Stern III**, never saw himself as my mentor, but was more my friend and partner in a practice in Southeastern, Wisconsin. I learned that practicing law brought a variety of issues and stories into your offices every single day. From those dying from inflictions I had never heard of, to the criminal element that at times, was disgusting and yet entitled to a quality representation.

Walter, if you are reading this, then you know that you were more to me than a partner and I can never thank you enough for the education you gave me, light years beyond that I encountered studying law. You taught me the moral and ethical aspects to a legal system that is in its waning years, I am afraid. We shall have those memories until our lights go out.

Thank you and I hope I have not disappointed you here.

✡ **Shalom Walter!**

daniel

1 Introduction

It is well settled that most criminal cases in the federal system, result in Plea Agreements. These are considered "contracts", between the United States and the defendant and are governed under contract principals. The pitfalls to these contracts, sometimes referred to as "Dealing with the Devil", require a layman's guide to the complicated and often frustrating process that causes their confinement in a mechanism called, The Federal Bureau of Prisons.

Read carefully, ask your attorney questions and when in doubt, ask the judge <u>before</u> you plead guilty. **It could cost you your soul!**

2 General Law of Plea Agreements

A defendant who is considering a plea is usually concerned about what he or she will plead guilty to and what penalties will be assessed. Although the shape of the plea is controlled by many fact-specific factors related to the crime and the defendant, there are some general principles of law and policy that impact on (1) the prosecutor s initial charging decision, (2) the amount of prosecutorial discretion available for bargaining, (3) the involvement of the court in the bargaining process, and (4) the defendant s ability to enforce the plea bargain once it is entered into. These general matters are the subject of this section. Specific ramifications of the various kinds of plea bargains available in federal court are covered in Section 3.

Plea bargains are controlled or influenced by various sources of law. Federal court practitioners are familiar with Rule 11 of the Federal Rules of Criminal Procedure (FRCrP), which, together with case law interpretations, sets out much of the basic law on plea bargaining. Certain portions of the Federal Sentencing Guidelines (USSG or Guidelines) in particular §1B1.2-4 on Relevant Conduct and §6B1 on Plea Agreements also have a strong effect on plea bargains. Probably the least familiar source of information is the Department of Justice (DOJ) Manual. Most of the DOJ policies discussed in this article are contained in Title 9, Chapter 27 of the DOJ Criminal Resource Manual at 9-27.001 et seq. They will be referred to herein by their section numbers. Most of the provisions of the various DOJ Bluesheets and other memoranda referred to herein have been compiled into that chapter. Copies of the relevant portions of the DOJ Manual should be included as an appendix to this article. If they are not, they should be available in local court libraries and in local federal defender offices.

Federal Rules of Criminal Procedure-Rule 11-- Pleas

(a) Entering a Plea.

(1) *In General.* A defendant may plead not guilty, guilty, or (with the court's consent) nolo contendere.

(2) *Conditional Plea.* With the consent of the court and the government, a defendant may enter a conditional plea of guilty or nolo contendere, reserving in writing the right to have an appellate court review an adverse determination of a specified pretrial motion. A defendant who prevails on appeal may then withdraw the plea.

(3) *Nolo Contendere Plea.* Before accepting a plea of nolo contendere, the court must consider the parties' views and the public interest in the effective administration of justice.

(4) *Failure to Enter a Plea.* If a defendant refuses to enter a plea or if a defendant organization fails to appear, the court must enter a plea of not guilty.

(b) Considering and Accepting a Guilty or Nolo Contendere Plea.

(1) *Advising and Questioning the Defendant.* Before the court accepts a plea of guilty or nolo contendere, the defendant may be placed under oath, and the court must address the defendant personally in open court. During this address, the court must inform the defendant of, and determine that the defendant understands, the following:

(A) the government's right, in a prosecution for perjury or false statement, to use against the defendant any statement that the defendant gives under oath;

(B) the right to plead not guilty, or having already so pleaded, to persist in that plea;

(C) the right to a jury trial;

(D) the right to be represented by counsel—and if necessary have the court appoint counsel—at trial and at every other stage of the proceeding;

(E) the right at trial to confront and cross-examine adverse witnesses, to be protected from compelled self-incrimination, to testify and present evidence, and to compel the attendance of witnesses;

10

(F) the defendant's waiver of these trial rights if the court accepts a plea of guilty or nolo contendere;

(G) the nature of each charge to which the defendant is pleading;

(H) any maximum possible penalty, including imprisonment, fine, and term of supervised release;

(I) any mandatory minimum penalty;

(J) any applicable forfeiture;

(K) the court's authority to order restitution;

(L) the court's obligation to impose a special assessment;

(M) in determining a sentence, the court's obligation to calculate the applicable sentencing-guideline range and to consider that range, possible departures under the Sentencing Guidelines, and other sentencing factors under 18 U.S.C. §3553(a);

(N) the terms of any plea-agreement provision waiving the right to appeal or to collaterally attack the sentence; and

(O) that, if convicted, a defendant who is not a United States citizen may be removed from the United States, denied citizenship, and denied admission to the United States in the future.

(2) *Ensuring That a Plea Is Voluntary.* Before accepting a plea of guilty or nolo contendere, the court must address the defendant personally in open court and determine that the plea is voluntary and did not result from force, threats, or promises (other than promises in a plea agreement).

(3) *Determining the Factual Basis for a Plea.* Before entering judgment on a guilty plea, the court must determine that there is a factual basis for the plea.

(c) Plea Agreement Procedure.

(1) *In General.* An attorney for the government and the defendant's attorney, or the defendant when proceeding pro se, may discuss and reach a plea agreement. The court must not participate in these discussions. If the defendant pleads guilty or nolo contendere to either a charged offense or a lesser or related offense, the plea agreement may specify that an attorney for the government will:

(A) not bring, or will move to dismiss, other charges;

(B) recommend, or agree not to oppose the defendant's request, that a particular sentence or sentencing range is appropriate or that a particular provision of the Sentencing Guidelines, or policy statement, or sentencing factor does or does not apply (such a recommendation or request does not bind the court); or

(C) agree that a specific sentence or sentencing range is the appropriate disposition of the case, or that a particular provision of the Sentencing Guidelines, or policy statement, or sentencing factor does or does not apply (such a recommendation or request binds the court once the court accepts the plea agreement).

(2) *Disclosing a Plea Agreement.* The parties must disclose the plea agreement in open court when the plea is offered, unless the court for good cause allows the parties to disclose the plea agreement in camera.

(3) *Judicial Consideration of a Plea Agreement.*

(A) To the extent the plea agreement is of the type specified in Rule 11(c)(1)(A) or (C), the court may accept the agreement, reject it, or defer a decision until the court has reviewed the presentence report.

(B) To the extent the plea agreement is of the type specified in Rule 11(c)(1)(B), the court must advise the defendant that the defendant has no right to withdraw the plea if the court does not follow the recommendation or request.

(4) *Accepting a Plea Agreement.* If the court accepts the plea agreement, it must inform the defendant that to the extent the plea agreement is of the type specified in Rule 11(c)(1)(A) or (C), the agreed disposition will be included in the judgment.

(5) *Rejecting a Plea Agreement.* If the court rejects a plea agreement containing provisions of the type specified in Rule 11(c)(1)(A) or (C), the court must do the following on the record and in open court (or, for good cause, in camera):

(A) inform the parties that the court rejects the plea agreement;

(B) advise the defendant personally that the court is not required to follow the plea agreement and give the defendant an opportunity to withdraw the plea; and

(C) advise the defendant personally that if the plea is not withdrawn, the court may dispose of the case less favorably toward the defendant than the plea agreement contemplated.

(d) Withdrawing a Guilty or Nolo Contendere Plea. A defendant may withdraw a plea of guilty or nolo contendere:

(1) before the court accepts the plea, for any reason or no reason; or

(2) after the court accepts the plea, but before it imposes sentence if:

(A) the court rejects a plea agreement under 11(c)(5); or

(B) the defendant can show a fair and just reason for requesting the withdrawal.

(e) Finality of a Guilty or Nolo Contendere Plea. After the court imposes sentence, the defendant may not withdraw a plea of guilty or nolo contendere, and the plea may be set aside only on direct appeal or collateral attack.

(f) Admissibility or Inadmissibility of a Plea, Plea Discussions, and Related Statements. The admissibility or inadmissibility of a plea, a plea discussion, and any related statement is governed by Federal Rule of Evidence 410.

(g) Recording the Proceedings. The proceedings during which the defendant enters a plea must be recorded by a court reporter or by a suitable recording device. If there is a guilty plea or a nolo contendere plea, the record must include the inquiries and advice to the defendant required under Rule 11(b) and (c).

(h) Harmless Error. A variance from the requirements of this rule is harmless error if it does not affect substantial rights.

2.1 Federal Rules of Criminal Procedure Rule 11

The *Federal Rules of Criminal Procedure*, hereinafter referred to as FRCrP, sets out the basic ground rules for all plea bargaining in federal court. Much of the case law regarding how the plea hearing is handled and the effects of various pleas is based on interpretation of Rule 11. It should be the first source consulted on any plea question. The following are some notable provisions of the rules. Citations to the rules in this section are to the FRCrP unless otherwise stated.

2.1.1 Types of pleas allowed under rules

Rule 11(a) describes the kinds of pleas allowed under the FRCrP as not guilty, guilty, and *nolo contendere*. In addition, a defendant may enter a conditional plea under **Rule 11(a)(2)** with the consent of the court and the government in order to preserve an issue for appeal. If the defendant prevails, he may withdraw the plea upon remand.

2.1.2 Advice to the defendant

Rule 11 spells out in some detail the proceedings that must occur for a guilty plea to be valid. Below is a checklist that can be used to determine whether all the bases were covered in a particular case. Note, however, that **Rule 11(h)** specifically provides that variance from the described procedure is harmless error if it does not affect substantial rights .

CLIENT CHECKLIST

Plea before Magistrate Judge

A Defendant must waive the right to proceed in front of district judge

Rule 7(b) (waiver of indictment)

Court must advise Defendant of nature of the charges

Court must advise Defendant about Grand Jury (16-23 jurors, 12 must agree)

RULE 11(b)(1) (advice to defendant)

(1) Defendant must be placed under oath

(1) Defendant must be personally addressed in open court

A - Government can use statements in perjury or false statement charges

B - Defendant can plead Not Guilty or persist in that pleading guilty

C - Right to jury trial (***Boykin v. Alabama***)

D - Right to counsel at trial and every other stage

D - Court will appoint counsel if necessary or requested by Defendant

E - Right to confront & cross-examine adverse witnesses (***Boykin***)

E - Right to remain silent (***Boykin***)

E - Right to testify

E - Right to subpoena witnesses

F - Plea of guilty or nolo waives trial, no trial will occur

G - Nature of charge

H - Maximum possible penalty: imprisonment, fine, supervision, restitution etc.

I - Mandatory minimum (if applicable)

J - Any applicable forfeiture

K - Court may order restitution

L - Court must impose special assessment

M - Court required to consider the applicable guidelines

M - Court may depart from guidelines

N - Terms of any waiver of appeal or collateral attack

Rule 11(b)(2) (voluntary plea)

Court must address Defendant personally in open court (***colloquy***)

Court must determine if plea is voluntary

Not the result of force or threats

Not the result of promises other than in Plea Agreement

Rule 11(b)(3) (factual basis)

Court must determine there is a factual basis for the plea

Rule 11(c) (plea agreement)

(1) The Court may not participate in plea negotiations

(2) The Parties must disclose plea in open court unless court permits otherwise

(3)(B) If recommendation, must advise that Defendant cannot withdraw plea once accepted

Rule 11(g) (recording)

The proceedings must be recorded by suitable method, court reporter audio recording

Rule 11(a)(3) (nolo contendere plea)

The Court must consider parties views & public interest in effective administration of justice

2.1.3 Types of plea agreements allowed under rules

Rule 11(c)(1) describes the kinds of pleas allowed under the FRCrP and provides that the government can:

(A) agree not to bring, or to dismiss, other charges in return for a plea,

(B) make a recommendation to the court, or agree not to oppose a defendant s recommendation, that a particular sentence or range is appropriate or that a particular guideline provision/policy/factor does or does not apply (non-binding),

(C) agree that a sentence or range is appropriate or that a particular guideline provision/policy/factor does or does not apply (binding once plea accepted).

2.1.4 Ability to withdraw from plea

Rule 11(c)(4) and **(5)** combine to allow the defendant to withdraw if a plea under 11(c)(1)(A) or 11(c)(1)(C) is rejected. In essence, this is a "back to square one" provision. Unfortunately, if the plea agreement includes a requirement that the defendant perform some action prior to the sentencing, it is difficult to get all the way back to square one. If a recommendation under **11(c)(1)(B)** is rejected, the defendant cannot withdraw under this rule. (emphasis added)

2.1.5 Involvement of Judges in Plea Negotiations

In general, **Rule 11(c)(1)** forbids the court to participate in any [plea bargaining] discussion. For example, a meeting of the judge, prosecutor, defendant, and defense counsel in chambers, off the record, during which the judge said he followed the prosecutor s recommendation 90% of the time, required reversal under **Rule 11(c)(1)**. *U.S. v. Daigle*, 63 F.3d 346 (5th Cir. 1995). Similarly, where defendant
got cold feet at the change of plea hearing and the judge told him (1) that if he was tried on all three counts he would have to get 15 years, (2) that if he pled guilty he would get 10 years, and (3) that he should talk to his lawyer to see if that is what he really wanted to do, the court crossed the line into the realm of forbidden participation in plea bargaining. *U.S. v. Casallas*, 59 F.3d 1173 (11th Cir. 1995).

2.1.6 Use of statements made in failed plea discussions Rule 11(f) relies on Rule 410, *Federal Rules of Evidence (FRE)*, to determine the admissibility of pleas, plea discussions, or related statements. Thus, ordinarily, counsel need not worry about the use of such statements against the client except in the two situations specifically excepted by Rule 410: an exception providing a rule of completeness that allows the rest of the statement in where part of it is already in, and an exception for use in perjury prosecutions.

Unfortunately, the Supreme Court has held that the protection of these rules is presumptively waivable . *U.S. v. Mezzanatto*, 513 U.S. 196 (1995). The 9th Circuit had previously held that, except for the specific exceptions stated in the rules as noted above, the protection of the rules could not be waived. *U.S. v. Mezzanatto*, 998 F.2d 1452, 1454-1456 (9th Cir. 1993). The Supreme Court rejected the 9th Circuit s analysis and permitted proffer statements made in plea discussions to be used as prior inconsistent statements in cross-examination at trial and to be proved up by an agent who attended the proffer meeting, noting that such use was consistent with the wording of the waiver executed before the proffer.

Note that, recently, some judges have questioned the viability of a similar protection for statements made as part of a cooperation agreement. Such statements may not be used to increase a defendant s guideline range under U.S.S.G. 1B1.8(a), but some judges are suggesting that in a post-*Booker* world, they can be used to determine a reasonable sentence after the guidelines are calculated. *U.S. v. Mills*, 329 F.3d 24, 27-30 (1st Cir. 2003).

2.2 Federal Sentencing Guidelines

The Guidelines impact on plea bargaining in several ways, and have added a new dimension to the analysis of the benefits of any plea federal bargain.

Counsel can now see with some clarity the effect on the sentence that a particular bargain might have. The guidelines have also set up their own standard for when judges should accept or reject plea bargains. Finally, and perhaps most importantly, the guidelines have radically changed the way in which conduct in addition to the conduct involved in the offense of conviction so-called relevant conduct , including acquitted conduct is factored into the calculation of the sentence.

2.2.1 Standards for acceptance or rejection of plea

The Guideline standard for acceptance of plea agreements is set forth in **USSG §6B1.2**, a Policy Statement which has three sections dealing with the three distinct types of plea agreements authorized under Rule 11(c)(1): (a) dismissals and agreements not to prosecute, (b) non-binding recommendations and (c) specific sentence agreements. The ramifications of these Guideline sections are dealt with more fully below in Section 3 describing the particular kinds of bargains available.

2.2.2 Use of relevant conduct under guidelines

The concept of *relevant conduct* has its genesis in **USSG §1B1.3.** A detailed analysis of relevant conduct is too broad a topic to be addressed in this article, although more detail about the use of relevant conduct under specific types of plea bargains is given in Section 3. In general, relevant conduct includes all conduct that occurred during the commission of the offense of conviction, or during the preparation for or attempt to avoid detection or responsibility for that offense provided that the defendant aided, abetted, counseled, commanded, induced, procured, or willfully caused the conduct. **USSG §1B1.3(a)(1)(A).** If the offense was a joint criminal activity, conduct is relevant if it was in furtherance of the activity and was reasonably foreseeable. **USSG §1B1.3(a)(1)(B).** The rules are different in a *groupable* offense as defined in **USSG §3D1.2(d)** the seriousness of which is usually measured in a

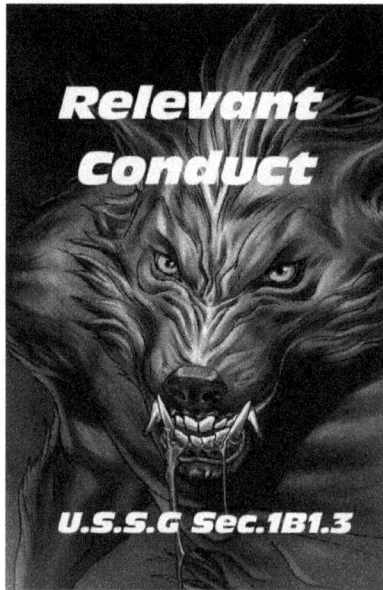

quantity like weight of drugs or number of dollars. In those cases relevant conduct also includes conduct that was part of a common scheme or plan with the offense of conviction. **USSG §1B1.3(a)(2).** Regardless of the type of offense, relevant conduct also includes all harm flowing from any of the above-described conduct, **USSG §1B1.3(a)(3),** and any special items specifically identified in the applicable guideline. **USSG §1B1.3(a)(4).**

Obviously this is a very broad definition, particularly in conspiracy cases. The problem facing the defense lawyer is that determination of the guideline range in a particular case is a multi-stage process, with relevant conduct being considered in different ways at different stages. Initially, a specific guideline from Chapter 2 where there is a guideline for each general type of offense is selected to be used as a basis for calculation based on the offense of conviction without regard to relevant conduct. **USSG §1B1.2(a)**. Within that chosen guideline, the base offense level and the applicability of various specific offense characteristics and cross references are all based on relevant conduct. USSG §1B1.2(b),3(a). Adjustments under Chapter 3 for things like role in the offense, obstruction of justice, or acceptance of responsibility are also based on relevant conduct. **USSG §1B1.3(a).** It is usually fair to assume that relevant conduct can and will be considered by the judge in one form or another at sentencing. This can sometimes negate the value of a plea bargain, although the defendant can often derive substantial benefit from the application of a particular guideline based on pleading to a particular charge. The defendant may also benefit from the removal of certain relevant conduct from the sentencing calculus because of the dismissal of some charges, at least in the 9th Circuit.

2.2.3 Use of acquitted conduct under guidelines

The rationale for allowing conduct for which defendant was acquitted to be considered at sentencing is that there is a different burden of proof, preponderance of the evidence, in effect at sentencing. *U.S. v. Carreon*, 11 F.3d 1225 (5th Cir. 1994) (conviction requires proof beyond a reasonable doubt, sentencing facts need only be proven by a preponderance of the evidence); U.S. v. Lawrence, 934 F.2d 868 (7th Cir.1991); *U.S. v. Fonner*, 920 F.2d 1330 (7th Cir.1990); *U.S. v. Smith*, 953 F.2d 1060 (7th Cir.1992); *U.S. v. Manor*, 936 F.2d 1238 (11th Cir.1991). Until 1996, the 9th Circuit did not allow the use of acquitted conduct at sentencing, *U.S. v. Brady*, 928 F.2d 844 (9th Cir. 1991), although counts on which the jury hung *could* be used. *U.S. v. Duran*, 15 F.3d 131 (9th Cir. 1994). Some judges in other circuits also felt strongly that use of acquitted conduct "must be modified [because a] just system of criminal sentencing cannot fail to distinguish between an allegation of conduct resulting in a conviction and an allegation of conduct resulting in an acquittal." *U.S. v. Conception*, 983 F.2d 369, 396 (2d Cir. 1992), cert. denied, 114 S. Ct. 163 (Newman, J., dissenting).

Although until the mid-90s there was some controversy about the use of acquitted conduct to enhance sentences, this came to an end when the Supreme Court held that acquitted conduct *can* be used in sentencing guideline calculations. *U.S. v. Watts*, 519 U.S. 148 (1997). The court followed the usual reasoning, holding that acquittal does not mean innocence, it merely means there exists a reasonable doubt. (see also, *United States v. Horne,* 474 F.3d 1004, 1006 (7th Cir. 2007).

2.3 Department of Justice (DOJ) Policies

Although DOJ policies do not impact directly on the court and do not create a right in the defendant to certain treatment, they do impact on the decisions made by the prosecutor. Knowledge of these policies knowing what the prosecutor can and cannot consider can assist the defense lawyer in framing arguments during the plea bargaining stage.

2.3.1 Policies affecting the charging decision

Since pre-guideline days, prosecutors have been directed to bring to the Grand Jury the most serious offense that is consistent with the nature of the defendant s conduct, and that is likely to result in a sustainable conviction. Principals of Federal Prosecution, July 1980; DOJ Manual at 9-27.001 et seq. A Justice Department Bluesheet dated March 13, 1989 reiterated that requirement, which is now codified at DOJ Manual 9-27.310. The prosecutor can charge other offenses as well, in addition to the most severe, if needed to reflect the nature of the conduct, provide an appropriate sentence, or strengthen the government's case.

Policies set forth in the **Thornburgh Bluesheet** dated June 16, 1989 emphasized the requirement that prosecutors file gun counts and Informations alleging prior convictions under 21 U.S.C. 851 to enhance penalties. The annotation at DOJ Manuel 9-27.750A adds more emphasis to the requirement with its description of "*Project Triggerlock*".

The **Reno Bluesheet** dated October 12, 1993 appeared on its face to loosen up the most serious readily provable charge requirement. (DOJ Manual 9-27.750B). In particular, it stated that it was appropriate for the prosecutor to consider the sentencing guideline range of a contemplated charge, whether the penalty would be proportional to the seriousness of the defendant s conduct, and whether the charge achieved the purposes of punishment, protection, deterrence and rehabilitation. Unfortunately, in response to an attack by Senator Hatch, Attorney General Reno clarified the Bluesheet by saying that it is still DOJ policy that prosecutors charge the most serious offense that is consistent with the conduct and likely to result in a sustainable conviction. In the wake of that clarification , many people felt that the Reno Bluesheet was no longer of any effect. **Ashcroft Memorandum:** More recently, DOJ has published the Ashcroft Memorandum of September 22, 2003, which either has been or will be turned into a Bluesheet in due time. The Ashcroft Memorandum sets out new policies for charging and plea bargaining, and is included as a appendix to this article. The new policy says that federal prosecutors must charge and pursue the most serious, readily provable offense or offenses that are supported by the facts of the case, except as authorized by designated supervisors. Most serious means those that generate the most substantial sentence, either under the Sentencing Guidelines or because of a mandatory minimum sentence. Charges are readily provable unless the prosecutor has a good faith doubt, for legal or evidentiary reasons, as to the Government s ability readily to prove a charge at trial. Once filed, the most serious readily provable charges may not be dismissed except to the extent permitted by later sections of the memorandum dealing primarily with charges that have no effect on the sentence, fast-track programs, reassessment of the evidence, or substantial assistance. There is, however, a special section devoted to dropping statutory enhancements like *21 U.S.C. § 851 or 18 U.S.C. § 924(c)* where they might cause the defendant to have no incentive to plead, and another section that recognizes resource constraints as legitimate reasons to decline or dismiss some charges.

2.3.2 Policies affecting plea bargaining

The 1980 Principles of Federal Prosecution set out a list of things the prosecutor can consider in reaching a plea bargain, including: cooperation, criminal history, seriousness of offense, remorse or acceptance of responsibility, fact that plea is quick and sure for government, probabilities at trial, effect on witnesses, probable sentence at trial, public interest in trial instead of plea, expense of trial and appeal, and effect of this plea on resolving other related or non-related cases. (DOJ Manual 9-27.420). Unfortunately, it is unclear how many of these factors remain viable in light of the later Bluesheets in the guideline era. The Thornburgh Bluesheet notes that after indictment, prosecutors are bargaining about charges that they have *already determined to be readily provable* and reflective of the seriousness of the defendant's conduct, and thus should rarely be in a position to drop charges. However, that same Bluesheet goes on to note that circumstances can arise, such as the need to protect a witness, that might change the bargaining calculus. Nonetheless, the thrust of all the policies was clear: charges are easy to make, hard to drop. **Ashcroft Memorandum:** In the Ashcroft Memorandum of September 22, 2003, sets out specific guidance for both charge bargaining and sentence bargaining. Charge bargaining is limited to dropping those charges that could be dropped under the rules set out in the previous section. Sentence bargaining is limited to sentences within the guideline range, or to a limited set of departures. Approved departures include those for substantial assistance and those under fast-track programs. Any other departure should be a rare occurrence, and prosecutors are required to oppose departures not supported by facts and law and are forbidden to stand silent.

2.4 Enforcement of Plea Agreements

In general, the terms of a plea agreement are "contractual in nature" and disputes will be "determined by objective standards". *U.S. v. Goroza*, 941 F.2d 905 (9th Cir. 1991). Any government promises that are part of the inducement to plead must be fulfilled. *Santobello v. New York*, 404 U.S. 257,262 (1971). However, plea agreements . . . are unique contracts in which special due process concerns for fairness and the adequacy of procedural safeguards obtain. *U.S. v. Carnine*, 974 F.2d 924, 928 (7th Cir. 1992). This is in part because courts are aware that a plea agreement is often a contract of adhesion. As a practical matter, the government has bargaining power utterly superior to that of the average defendant if only because the precise charge or charges to be brought and thus the ultimate sentence to be imposed under the guidelines scheme is up to the prosecution. *U.S. v. Johnson*, 992 F. Supp. 437, 439-40 (D.D.C. 1997). Thus, [c]ourts construe plea agreements strictly against the Government. This is done for a variety of reasons, before the indictment is handed up. It noted that whether bargaining takes place before or after indictment, the Department policy is the same, but it also recognized that it will be difficult for anyone other than the prosecutor and the defendant to know whether, prior to the indictment, the prosecutor bargained in conformity with the Department s policy. The 2003 Ashcroft Memorandum does not contain this caveat, but in practice, it is still possible to avoid more serious charges by getting with the prosecutor early and arranging a pre-indictment plea. If nothing else, you can try to influence the prosecutor s view of what is readily provable.

3.2 Charge Bargaining

Charge bargaining the agreement to dismiss or not charge certain counts, or to substitute a less serious charge for a more serious one is one of the most effective bargaining tools. Absent extremely unusual circumstances, judges cannot prevent the prosecution from dismissing charges and can never force them to file charges. Charge bargaining is limited by the DOJ policies mentioned in Section 2.3.2

above, but is widespread in practice.

Sample Plea Agreement Language

*Pursuant to Fed.R.Crim.P. **11(c)(1)(A)**, the government agrees to dismiss counts 2-7. Insofar as the District of Arizona has venue over such matters, the government agrees not to prosecute the following charges: Robbery of the Valley National Bank at 200 N. Central, Phoenix, Arizona on January 16, 2003.*

3.2.1 Rules and Guidelines

Agreements to dismiss or not to pursue charges are authorized under Rule 11(c)(1)(A). In the usual case, an agreement not to prosecute a defendant on other criminal charges is binding only in those judicial districts identified in the plea agreement. ***U.S. v. Phibbs***, 999 F.2d 1053, 1081-82 (6th Cir. 1993). The court is required to advise the defendant that it may reject the agreements, and that defendant can withdraw if that

27

occurs. **Rule 11(c)(3)(A). USSG §6B1.2(a)** advises the court to accept such agreements if the court determines for reasons stated on the record, that the remaining charges adequately reflect the seriousness of the actual offense behavior and that accepting the agreement will not undermine the statutory purposes of sentencing or the sentencing guidelines. Just what it means to adequately reflect the seriousness of the offense behavior is unclear. The 1989 Thornburgh Memorandum cites the example of dropping charges that would not have any effect on the guideline range. (DOJ Manual 9-27.410). This extremely narrow construction is not very helpful to the defense.

3.2.2 DOJ policies

In general, as mentioned in Section 3.1 above, DOJ frowns on dismissing readily provable charges that reflect the seriousness of the defendant s conduct. DOJ Manual 9-27.400. Surprisingly, the 1989 Thornburgh Memorandum suggested that prosecutors may drop readily provable charges in order to effectuate aims of the criminal justice system other than observance of the guidelines, such as the conservation of resources. The example given was the dropping of a case because it would be too time consuming or would interfere with the prosecution of other cases. (DOJ Manual 9-27.400). The 2003 Ashcroft Memorandum continues this reasoning with permission to drop statutory enhancements like *21 U.S.C. § 851 or 18 U.S.C. § 924(c)* where they might cause the defendant to have no incentive to plead, or to drop charges based on resource constraints. Unfortunately, this principle is not reflected in the Sentencing Guidelines Policy Statements in USSG Chapter 6. The DOJ manual contains a separate treatment of non-prosecution agreements that are made in return for cooperation. Counsel pursuing such

agreement should refer to §9-27.600. In particular, §9-27.641 sets forth the process for obtaining such an agreement where the offenses where in multiple districts. (*U.S. Attorneys-Criminal Resource Manual-Section 9* is annexed hereto as **Appendix "A"**)

3.2.3 Effect of plea on maximum sentence available

Even under the Guidelines, the court is limited to the statutory maximum sentence for the offense or offenses of conviction. In some cases, the consideration of relevant conduct under the Guidelines, along with the application of various upward departures, may drive the guideline range to an unacceptable height. Although it is difficult to control guideline calculations, pleading to an offense with a maximum of five years as opposed to one with a maximum of ten years at least gives the client some protection.

3.2.4 Use of dismissed and uncharged conduct under guidelines

The guideline sentencing range and the eventual sentence in a particular case are influenced by the selection of the appropriate guideline to serve as the basis for calculation, the decision to apply various adjustments to that guideline based on analysis of the conduct relevant to the offense of conviction, the determination of the defendant s criminal history category, and the decision to effect an upward departure. The effect on each of these of a bargain dismissing charges is discussed below. The general rules regarding the use of *relevant conduct* are discussed in Section 2.2.2.

3.2.4.1 Selecting the appropriate guideline section

Although almost all relevant conduct can be considered in some form at sentencing, USSG §1B1.2 & 3, the selection of the actual *guideline section* to be applied is determined by the charge of *conviction*. **USSG §1B1.2(a)**. The defendant can often derive some benefit from having the choice of guideline, and thus the base offense level, based on conviction for a particular charge. Other relevant conduct is then relegated to consideration only in terms of specific offense characteristics or possible departures. Thus a plea agreement can be effective by preventing the use of dismissed counts in deciding which guideline to apply.

The guideline benefit of pleading to a lesser charge can be nullified if the oral or written plea agreement contains a stipulation that specifically establishes a more serious offense. In such cases, the court may apply the guideline appropriate to the more serious conduct. **USSG §1B1.2(a) & (c).** However, such a stipulation takes effect only if the defendant and government explicitly agree that it is to be used for that purpose. **USSG §1B1.2, comment. (n.1).**

Counsel should also be alert to the possibility of a cross reference to another guideline. For example, the guideline on obstructing or impeding officers, USSG §2A2.4, refers the court to the assault guideline, **USSG §2A2.2**, if the conduct constituted aggravated assault .

3.2.4.2 Determining the guideline range

USSG §1B1.3 provides that, once the appropriate guideline section has been selected based on the offense of conviction, all *relevant conduct* should be used to determine the applicability of specific offense characteristics, cross-references, and adjustments and thus the actual guideline range under the chosen guideline. Conduct that constitutes or is related to counts that are dismissed or not charged pursuant to a plea bargain can still influence the guideline calculation if that conduct is found to be relevant to the offense of conviction. The definition of *relevant conduct* is discussed more fully in Section 2.2.2, but in general it includes: all conduct that the defendant aided, abetted or was otherwise personally responsible for, conduct in a joint criminal activity that was foreseeable and in furtherance of the activity, and conduct in a *groupable* offense that was part of a common scheme or plan with the offense of conviction. This is a very broad definition, particularly in conspiracy cases. The general rule is that counts dismissed as part of a plea agreement *will* be used to calculate the defendant's sentence if the counts are part of the same course of conduct to which the defendant pled guilty. *79 Cornell L. Rev. 299, n.160 citing U.S. v. Frierson*, 945 F.2d 650, 653-55 (3d Cir. 1991), *cert. denied*, 503 U.S. 952 (1992); *U.S. v. Smallwood*, 920 F.2d 1231, 1239 (5th Cir. 1991), *cert. denied*, 501 U.S. 1238 (1991); *U.S. v. Taplette*, 872 F.2d 101 (5th Cir. 1989), *cert. denied*, 493 U.S. 841 (1989); *U.S. v. Rodriguez-Nuez*, 919 F.2d 461, 464-65 (7th Cir. 1990); *U.S. v. Williams*, 880 F.2d 804, 805-06 (4th Cir. 1989); *U.S. v. Scroggins*, 880 F.2d 1204, 1213-14 (11th Cir. 1989), *cert. denied*, 494 U.S. 1083 (1990); *U.S. v. Wright*, 873 F.2d 437, 440-41 (1st Cir. 1989); *U.S. v. Sailes*, 872 F.2d 735, 738-39 (6th

Cir. 1989); *U.S. v. Baird*, 109 F.3d 856, 865 (3rd Cir. 1997). *But see **U.S. v. Griggs***, 71 F.3d 276 (8th Cir. 1996) (uncharged conduct can be considered in determining the base offense level for drug cases *unless* the plea agreement limits the court to the stipulated facts in the plea).

Not all circuits thought that it was fair to use dismissed counts in calculating the sentencing guideline range. The 9th Circuit prohibited such use, based in part on analysis of a since-changed version of the plea bargaining guideline, **USSG §6B1.2(a),** and in part on the heretical idea that the defendant should get the benefit of his bargain. *U.S. v. Castro-Cervantes*, 927 F.2d 1079 (9th Cir. 1990). **USSG §6B1.2(a)** was amended effective 11/1/92 to specifically provide that both dismissed charges and charges not filed pursuant to a plea agreement *can* be considered as relevant conduct under **§1B1.3**. Even in the 9th Circuit, the rationale of Castro-Cervantes was not extended to offenses that are *groupable* under the aggregate harm analysis of **USSG §3D1.2**. Therefore, if the level of an offense depends on some quantity such as the weight of drugs or the number of dollars involved in a fraud, such that it would be groupable under §3D1.2, then the quantities involved in the dismissed counts *will* be considered in determining the guidelines. *U.S. v. Fine*, 975 F.2d 596 (9th Cir. 1992) (en banc).

3.2.4.3 Determining the criminal history category

In general, counts dismissed pursuant to a plea agreement are not considered in the calculation of the criminal history category in the instant case. However, as discussed in **Section 3.2.4.4,** upward departures for inadequacy of criminal history under **§4A1.3** are governed by much the same principles as other upward departures, and thus the dismissed counts might well be considered for this purpose depending on circuit law. Some circuits have specifically permitted departures under **USSG §4A1.3** based on dismissed conduct. *U.S. v. Ashburn*, 38 F.3d 803 (5th Cir. 1994) (*en banc*); *U.S. v. Collins*, 104 F.3d 1436 (8th Cir. 1997). Note also that counts dismissed in one case might also be considered for upward departure in a separate case. *U.S. v. Ruffin*, 997 F.2d 343 (7th Cir.1993)

3.2.4.4 Deciding on a sentence or a departure

Under the guideline scheme, almost any information may be considered in determining the exact sentence within a guideline range or the propriety or extent of a departure under **USSG §1B1.4.**

Prior to 2000, there was a split on whether it was appropriate to use conduct underlying dismissed charges to support a departure. For example, in the 9th Circuit dismissed counts could not be used as a basis for upward departure. *U.S. v. Castro-Cervantes*, 927 F.2d 1079 (9th Cir. 1990). Nor can uncharged counts be used for that purpose. *U.S. v. Faulkner*, 952 F.2d 1066 (9th Cir. 1991). Other circuits embraced upward departures based on dismissed conduct more readily, particularly since Watts was decided. *See* *U.S. v. Kim*, 896 F.2d 678, 684 (2nd Cir.1990) (dismissed counts can be used in some circumstances); *U.S. v. Ashburn*, 38 F.3d 803, 807 (5th Cir.1994) (same); *U.S. v. Zamarripa*, 905 F.2d 337, 341 (10th Cir.1990) (same). In 2000, the guidelines were amended to add §5K2.21, which specifically provides for departures based on dismissed or uncharged conduct. After that, even the 9th Circuit has held that the amendment effectively supercedes the prohibition and that used of dismissed or uncharged conduct is permissible. *U.S. v. Barragan-Espinosa*, 350 F.3d 978, 983 (9th Cir. 2003).

3.3 Recommendation Bargaining

Recommendation bargaining the entering of a plea in return for a simple non-binding recommendation from the prosecutor gives the defendant less than any other bargain. Sometimes, however, it is the best that can be done. When coupled with strong knowledge of the judge and probation officer it can yield great benefit.

Sample Plea Agreement Language

*Pursuant to **Fed.R.Crim.P.** 11(c)(1)(B), the United States and the defendant agree as follows: a) The United States will recommend that defendant receive no adjustment for his role in the offense, and that a sentence of 24 to 36 months imprisonment is appropriate; b) Supervised release and fines shall be determined by the court.*

3.3.1 Rules and Guidelines

Non-binding recommendations are authorized under **Rule 11(c)(1)(B). USSG §6B1.2(b)** authorizes, but does not require, the court to accept the recommendation if it is within the applicable guideline range or departs for justifiable reasons . When confronted with a recommendation or a cap below the guidelines, some courts simply recite the mantra that the sentence departs for justifiable reasons and go ahead and accept the deal. Unfortunately, the commentary to **USSG §6B1.2(b)** notes that departing for *justifiable reasons* actually means that such departure is authorized by **18 U.S.C. §3553(b)**. That statute requires the court to impose a sentence *within* the guideline range unless there exists an aggravating or mitigating circumstance not adequately considered by the Sentencing Commission. In otherwords, the words justifiable reasons in the Guideline do not create a new reason for departure the facts of the case must be sufficient to justify a departure under the normal rules. Where there is no right to withdraw from a plea such as where the plea agreement is for a recommendation under **Rule 11(c)(1)(B)** the court should advise the defendant that he has no right to withdraw if the government s recommendation is rejected. Rule 11(c)(3)(B). Failure to so advise has been held to be reversible error unless the record shows that the defendant possessed that knowledge. *U.S. v. Graibe*, 946 F.2d 1428 (9th Cir. 1991). However, there are a number of exceptions. For example, failure to advise the defendant that she would not be allowed to withdraw her guilty plea if the court rejected the government s sentencing recommendation was error, but when the court did in fact follow the recommendation, there was no prejudice and the sentence was affirmed. *U.S. v. Chan*, 82 F.3d 921, *opinion amended and superseded by* 97 f.3d 1582 (9th Cir. 1996). A similar failure to advise the defendant during the colloquy was harmless where, at sentencing, the court became aware of the problem and gave the defendant the opportunity to withdraw and the defendant refused. *U.S. v. Diaz-Vargas*, 35 F.3d 1221 (7th Cir. 1994).

3.3.2 DOJ policies

The 1989 Thornburgh Bluesheet seems to give carte blanche for recommendations of sentences within the guideline range and recommendations for acceptance of responsibility. Recommendation of departures is discouraged, other than **USSG §5K.1** departures for substantial assistance. In the Ashcroft Memorandum of September 22, 2003, recommendation bargaining is limited to sentences within the guideline range, or to a limited set of departures. Approved departures include those for substantial assistance and those under fast-track programs. Any other departure should be a rare occurrence, and prosecutors are required to oppose departures not supported by facts and law and are forbidden to stand silent. **DOJ Manual 9-27.730** states that recommendations should only be made when a plea agreement requires it or the public interest warrants it. The text is fairly even-handed it even states that a prosecutor should make a recommendation if the prosecutor feels that otherwise it is likely that the sentence will be unfair to the defendant. However, the listing of considerations to be weighed in making a recommendation, are heavily weighted toward the government. DOJ Manual 9-27.745.

The listing of things to take into account in determining whether to enter into a plea bargain at all is much more extensive and useful to the defense. DOJ Manual 9-27.420. The DOJ manual does not make a big distinction between recommendations and stipulations, but it draws a bright line between recommendations that are in the guideline range and those that are not. DOJ Manual 9-27.410.

3.3.3 Effect of recommendation below the guideline range

The Guidelines require the court to reject a plea outside the guideline range unless there is justification for a departure under *18 U.S.C. 3553(b)* and the Guidelines themselves. **USSG §6B1.2(c)(2)** and Commentary. Nonetheless, if the court does accept a recommendation and sentence below the guideline range, that decision *may* be shielded from appellate scrutiny by the doctrine of waiver. After all, the fact that the prosecution has recommended the sentence should lead the court and the defendant to reasonably expect that the government would not appeal the sentence. This result would be troubling for the appellate courts because the parties would in effect create their own self-help departure scheme. Courts have held in numerous cases that a *defendant* waives any objection that he fails to make in the district court. See, e.g., *U.S. v. Belden,* 957 F.2d 671 (9th Cir. 1992), *cert. denied*, 506 U.S. 882 (1992); *U.S. v. Bafia*, 949 F.2d 1465, 1476 (7th Cir.1991) (defendant waived objections to enhancement for obstruction of justice and denial of departure for acceptance of responsibility by failing to object at sentencing). One would expect the same rule to apply to the *government*. The 11th Circuit so held where the prosecutor agreed that the court had discretion and did not object to downward departure. *U.S. v. Prickett,* 898 F.2d 130 (11th Cir. 1990). However, the 9th Circuit has found an exception to allow the government to appeal where there was plain error and "injustice". *U.S. v. Snider*, 957 F.2d 703 (9th Cir. 1992). *Accord, U.S. v. Perkins*, 108 F.3d 512 (4th Cir. 1997) (plain error rule allows review of unwarranted downward departure in order to protect integrity of judicial system).

For other exceptions to the rule against raising issues for the first time on appeal see *U.S. v. Flores-Payon*, 942 F.2d 556, 558 (9th Cir.1991) (exceptions to general rule exist for exceptional circumstances, change in law during appeal, issue is purely one of law and other party not prejudiced, and plain error and injustice). What constitutes plain error varies from place to place. See *U.S. v. Fant*, 974 F.2d 559, 565 (4th Cir.1992) (plain error results when prosecutor breaches plea agreement); *U.S. v. Goldfaden*, 959 F.2d 1324, 1328 (5th Cir.1992) (same); *U.S. v. Phillips*, 37 F.3d 1210 (7th Cir.1994) (no plain error where plea agreement breached) Also of relevance are *U.S. v. Hand*, 913 F.2d 854, 856 n.2 (10th Cir.1990) (breach of plea agreement may be raised for first time on appeal) and *U.S. v. Moscahlaidis*, 868 F.2d 1357, 1360 (3rdCir.1989) (same).

3.3.4 Effect of government failure to make recommendation

The government s failure to recommend a sentence at the low end of the guideline range, as called for by the plea agreement, called for a reversal even where, in response to the court s question, the prosecutor admitted that she was recommending the low end. In reversing, the court noted that the harmless error rule does not apply to the law of contractual plea agreements. *U.S. v. Myers*, 32 F.3d 411, 413 (9th Cir. 1994) (situation aggravated by the fact that the prosecutor drew the court s attention to facts justifying a higher sentence, and that the defense attorney s objections, the court s question, and the prosecutor s acknowledgment of the agreement all came after the sentence had been passed). *Accord, U.S. v. Hawley*, 99 F.3d 682 (10th Cir. 1996) (defendant entitled to relief regardless of whether the government s conduct actually affected the sentencing judge). A contrary result obtained in a case where the written plea agreement contained the substance of the government s recommendation and the appellate court felt

38

that if the government had made the recommendation in court at the time of sentencing it would not have likely changed defendants sentence . *U.S. v. Flores-Sandoval*, 94 F.3d 346 (7th Cir. 1996).

An agreement to recommend a sentence does not imply an obligation to do so enthusiastically or to set forth on the record the reasons for the recommendation. *U.S. v. Benchimol*, 471 U.S. 453, 455-456 (1985). Nonetheless, the prosecutor may not pay lip service to the agreement with a recommendation but undermine that recommendation by supporting the higher presentence report guideline calculation in a sentencing memo. *U.S. v. Taylor*, 77 F.3d 368 (11th Cir. 1996). *See also U.S. v. Canada*, 960 F.2d 263 (1st Cir. 1992) (ordering specific performance via resentencing and noting that while the recommendation need not be made with any particular degree of enthusiasm, nonetheless it is unfair for the prosecutor to inject material reservations about an agreement to which the government has committed itself.) Where defendant pleaded guilty in federal court in Wyoming with an agreement that the government would recommend *concurrent* time with an upcoming federal sentencing in Iowa, and where the government attorney in Iowa in fact requested a *consecutive* sentence, the defendant was entitled to specific performance from the government because absent an express limitation, any promises made by an AUSA in one district will bind an AUSA in another district. *U.S. v. Van Thournout*, 100 F.3d 590 (8th Cir. 1996). Apparently, even an impossible promise must be kept. Where the government agreed to recommend probation but probation was not permissible under the guidelines, and the government informed the court that it was not bound to impose a sentence that would be illegal under the guidelines , the plea bargain was based on an unfulfillable promise and the defendant should be allowed to withdraw his plea. *U.S. v. Cooper*, 70 F.3d 563 (10th Cir. 1995).

3.4 Stipulation Bargaining

Stipulation bargaining the entering of a plea in return for a binding recommendation is the holy grail of plea bargaining in federal court. Armed with a stipulated sentence a client can be assured of what is going to happen, unless the judge rejects the plea altogether.

Sample Plea Agreement Language

*Pursuant to **Fed.R.Crim.P.** 11(c)(1)(C), the United States and the defendant stipulate and agree that the following is an appropriate sentence: a) The parties stipulate that defendant shall not receive an adjustment for role in the offense and shall receive a maximum of 60 months imprisonment. b) Supervised release and fines shall be determined by the court. c) If the court, after reviewing this plea agreement, and before accepting it, concludes that any provision is inappropriate, it may reject the plea agreement, giving the defendant, in accordance with **Fed.R.Crim.P.** 11(c)(5), an opportunity to withdraw the guilty plea. d) Pursuant to Sentencing Guidelines §6B1.1(c), the court shall defer acceptance or rejection of this plea agreement until there has been an opportunity to consider the presentence report.*

3.4.1 Rules and guidelines

Bargaining for stipulated sentences is authorized under **Rule 11 (c)(1)(C)** and is analyzed for Sentencing Guidelines purposes under

40

§6B1.2(c). The guideline standard is the same as that for a recommended sentence discussed in Section 3.3.1 the judge may accept the agreement if the sentence is within the guideline range or departs for justifiable reasons , meaning that there is a legally sufficient reason for departure. **Rule 11(c)(5),** referred to in the sample plea agreement language above, refers to the right to withdraw provided by the rules and the guidelines in the case of **Rule 11(c)(1)(A)** and **11(c)(1)(C)** agreements. <u>As noted previously, this is a back to square one provision that attempts to allow both parties to go back to the *status quo ante*. This is the only sense in which a plea agreement including a stipulation is *binding* on the court the court need not accept it, but the defendant will be allowed to withdraw if the court does not.</u>

3.4.2 DOJ policies

Stipulation bargaining is recognized under **DOJ Manual 9-27.410**, but little is said about it. The manual makes little distinction between recommendations and stipulations. Neither does the Ashcroft Memorandum of September 22, 2003, which limits stipulations in the same way it limits recommends, namely, to sentences within the guideline range, or to a limited set of departures. Approved departures include those for substantial assistance and those under fast-track programs. Any other departure should be a rare occurrence, and prosecutors are required to oppose departures not supported by facts and law and are forbidden to stand silent.

3.4.3 Sentence agreements under Rule 11(c)(1)(C)

Often the plea agreement will not stipulate an exact sentence, but will instead set forth a maximum often called a *cap* or a range of sentence. Prior to the amendments of 1999, the rule only provided for the stipulation of a specific sentence. There was some question about whether a cap or a range was a specific sentence under the rule. *Compare* **U.S. v. Bolinger**, 940 F.2d 478 (9th Cir.1991) *with* **U.S. v. Newsome**, 894 F.2d 852 (6th Cir. 1990). The range question is now obsolete, as the rule provides for stipulation of a sentencing range. The exact meaning of a cap for example, does the absence of a lower end imply that probation is possible or departure below the guidelines is agreed to? is a matter of local practice. As discussed in Section 3.3.3, supra, the court can always reject a plea under **Rule 11(c)(5)** and the guidelines require it to do so if the plea is outside the guideline range unless a departure is justified. However, if the agreement is under **Rule 11(c)(1)(C),** the court must either accept the agreement or allow the defendant to withdraw from the plea. Under these circumstances, the court is under some pressure
to go ahead and accept the agreement and sentence below the guideline range. The discussion in section 3.3.3 of a possible waiver of appeal by the government would also apply in this case.

3.5 Agreements Regarding Guideline Factors

The 1999 amendments to **Rule 11(c)(1)** now permit the government to recommend or stipulate whether a particular provision of the guidelines, policy statement, or sentencing factor applies in a particular case. Recommendations under **Rule 11(c)(1)(B)** are never binding, and defendant has no recourse if they are rejected by the court. Rejection of stipulations under **Rule 11(c)(1)(C)**, however, gives rise to a right to withdraw under will **Rule 11(c)(5).**

Sample Plea Agreement Language

> *The parties stipulate as follows: the offense did not involve more than minimal planning, and there are no role-in-the-offense, victim-related, obstruction, or Multiple-Count Sentencing*

Adjustments within the meaning of the Guidelines, Chapter 3.

3.5.1 Court must reject inaccurate stipulations

Generally, **USSG §6B1.4(d)** states that sentencing courts are not bound by stipulations in plea agreements but instead are free to determine the facts relevant to sentencing. The court may rely on the presentence report to determine the true facts. **USSG §6B1.4(d);** *U.S. v. Lutfiyya*, 26 F.3d 1468 (8th Cir. 1994). The fact that the government stipulated to certain facts in the plea agreement does not prevent the district court from considering conduct *outside* the stipulated facts, including uncharged conduct. *U.S. v. Griggs*, 71 F.3d 276 (8th Cir. 1995). However, if the government argues a position contrary to its stipulation as opposed to the judge simply rejecting it there may be a violation of the plea agreement. *U.S. v. Valencia*, 985 F.2d 758 (5th Cir. 1993).

3.5.2 Stipulations that hurt the defendant may be relied upon

Stipulations that go against the defendant can be relied by the court even if they are not supported by the presentence report apparently as admissions of a party. *U.S. v. Cambra*, 933 F.2d 752 (9th Cir. 1991) (stipulated to value of fraud loss); *U.S. v. Bos*, 917 F.2d 1178 (9th Cir. 1990) (stipulation to greater offense). Even stipulations regarding dismissed counts may be considered. *U.S. v. Saldana*, 12 F.3d 160 (9th Cir. 1993). In determining *relevant conduct* the district court could properly rely on stipulation in the plea agreement that certain conduct constitutes relevant conduct under § **1B1.3** of the guidelines . *U.S. v. Flores-Sandoval*, 94 F.3d 346 (7th Cir. 1996) (court ignores defense argument that some conduct not truly relevant , relying on stipulation that it *was* relevant). Similarly, defendant s stipulation that the abuse of trust enhancement should apply, coupled with an agreement not to appeal the accuracy of the stipulated facts, constituted a waiver of her right to appeal a finding based thereon. *U.S. v. Allison*, 59 F.3d 43 (6th Cir. 1995), *cert. denied*, 516 U.S. 1002 (1995). A stipulation may constitute a waiver, under appropriate circumstances, but does not relieve the court of its obligation to determine its own view of the facts and law. *U.S. v. Mankiewicz*, 122 F.3d 399, 403 n.1 (7th Cir. 1997).

3.6 Agreements Regarding Restitution

Restitution is not covered exhaustively here. The material in this section has not been updated in recent years. This section only attempts to point counsel toward some of the problems that may be encountered and toward some of the relevant law.

Sample Plea Agreement Language

> *Defendant specifically agrees to make restitution to the victim in the amount of $400,000 even though the defendant is not pleading guilty to and has not been convicted of the offense giving rise to the victims losses.*

3.6.1 Victim Witness Protection Act Prior to 1990

Restitution to the victim of the offense of conviction for amounts involved in the count of conviction has always been allowed. *18 U.S.C. 3651* (the Federal Probation Act or FPA) (repealed), *18 U.S.C. 3663 (the Victim Witness Protection Act or VWPA).* Restitution to persons who are not victims of the offense of conviction or for losses not resulting from the offense of conviction is more problematic.

Before the VWPA, restitution was ordered under the FPA which allowed restitution to *all* victims for *all* harms. *U.S. v. Hammer*, 967 F.2d 339 (9th Cir. 1992). The FPA was repealed November 1, 1987. The VWPA came into effect January 1, 1983 and appears to have overlapped with the FPA until the FPA was repealed. The VWPA applied only to Title 18 and certain sections of the Federal Aviation Act. *U.S. v.Snider*, 957 F.2d 703 (9th Cir. 1992). The VWPA only authorized restitution to the victim of the offense of conviction for the losses caused by the offense, and it did not allow restitution by agreement. *Hughey v. U.S.*, 495 U.S. 411 (1990).

3.6.2 Victim Witness Protection Act After 1990

As of November 29, 1990 the VWPA was amended to allow restitution in any criminal case "to the extent agreed by the parties in a plea agreement". This has been held not retroactive because of *ex post facto* problems. *U.S. v. Snider*, 957 F.2d 703 (9th Cir. 1992). Agreements to allow otherwise unenforceable restitution are a useful bargaining tool, but may create a situation where the defendant is certain to violate probation and end up back in custody.

3.6.3 Mandatory Victims Restitution Act of 1996

The *Mandatory Victims Restitution Act of 1996 (MVRA), 18 U.S.C. §3663A-3664*, a part of the Anti-Terrorism Act of 1996, has changed the face of restitution, mostly to the detriment of the defendant. The MVRA modified the VWPA and makes restitution mandatory, without regard to a defendant s economic situation. *U.S. v. Dubose*, 146 F.3d 1141 (9th Cir. June 26, 1998) (holding restitution under MVRA is punishment but does not violate the 8th Amendment prohibition against excessive fines or cruel and unusual punishment). By its terms, the MVRA applies in all but a few cases. 18 U.S.C. §3663(c)(3). Courts have split on whether mandatory restitution is punishment and thus subject to the Ex Post Facto Clause. *See U.S. v. Newman*, 144 F.3d 531 (7th Cir. 1998) (holding it does not violate Ex Post Facto Clause and characterizing cases from the 2nd, 9th and D.C. Circuits holding to the contrary as without reasoning); *Dubose*, (holding

46

restitution under MVRA is punishment but does not violate the 8th Amendment prohibition against excessive fines or cruel and unusual punishment). *Compare* **U.S. v. Baggett,** 125 F.3d 1319 (9th Cir. 1997) (stating that retrospective application of the MVRA violates the Ex Post Facto Clause).

3.6.4 Waiver of appeal regarding restitution

Where a plea agreement acknowledged that the court could order restitution of a certain amount, and the presentence report stated restitution was applicable, defendant s failure to object to the report or the restitution order was a waiver of the right to appeal the restitution. *U.S. v. Allison*, 59 F.3d 43 (6th Cir. 1995).

3.7 Agreements Involving Cooperation

Cooperation agreements usually require the defendant to perform some act in the future. As a result, they must be analyzed like complex employment contracts in order to determine exactly what the client will be required to do and what benefit or risk is involved. Cooperation agreements are often long and complex. The text of the cooperation portion of a sample plea agreement has been broken up and set forth under the relevant subheadings below..**7.1 Subject matter of cooperation**

Sample Plea Agreement Language

Self-incriminating information provided by the defendant during cooperation involving criminal activity for which he is charged, has not been charged, or will not be charged

> *pursuant to this agreement will not be used in determining defendant's applicable guideline range pursuant to Section 1B1.8 of the Sentencing Guidelines. The Guideline range will be calculated with the government's proof independent of defendant's cooperation.*

USSG §1B1.8(a) prevents the use of information provided by the defendant pursuant to a cooperation agreement to determine the guideline range *if the government has agreed not to use it*, as the government does in the sample agreement above. In the absence of a **USSG §1B1.8(a)** agreement not to use information, boilerplate language in a plea agreement saying that the government was free to provide all relevant information to the court at sentencing was held to override the **Rule 410** and Rule 11(f) protection of statements made during a proffer in plea negotiations, even though the proffer agreement itself provided that the information would not be used. *U.S. v. Fagge*, 101 F.3d 232 (2nd Cir. 1996). Note that the information cannot be used to determine the guideline range, but other uses such as upward departures are not specifically prohibited. Nonetheless, some courts have refused to allow the prosecution to use the information for any purpose that would result in a harsher sentence. *U.S. v. Malvito,* 946 F.2d 1066 (4th Cir. 1991); *U.S. v. Ledesma*, 979 F.2d 816, 820, n.6 (11th Cir.1992) (information divulged pursuant to plea agreement may not be used for upward departure). Recently, some courts have decided that although the information cannot be used to

determine the guideline range, it can and should be used to determine if a sentence is reasonable in a post-***Booker*** analysis. The courts are relying on 18 USC § 3661 which says that no limitation shall be placed on the information the court may receive and consider for purposes of sentencing. *See **U.S. v. Mills***, 329 F.3d 24 (1st Cir. 2003). Also, not all information provided by the defendant is protected. **USSG §1B1.8(b)** specifically allows use of the information if it was already know to the government, if it is about prior convictions and is used to determine criminal history or career offender status, if it is to be used in a perjury prosecutions, if there has been a breach by defendant, or to determine if a downward departure for substantial assistance is warranted. The information must have been provided as part of the cooperation. Statements made to a probation officer in a routine interview may not protected under **USSG §1B1.8(a)**. *United State v. Miller*, 910 F.2d 1321, 1325 (6th Cir. 1990); *U.S. v. Jarman*, 144 F.3d 912, 914-915 (6th Cir. 1998).

There is a distinction between information provided pursuant to a cooperation agreement and statements made during failed plea negotiations. Note that the protection of USSG §1B1.8(a) is contingent on government agreement, unlike the protections of **Rule 410**, **FRE**, and **Rule 11(f), FRCrP**, both of which prohibit the use of statements made in the course of plea discussions with an attorney for the prosecuting authority which do not result in a guilty plea.

3.7.5 Types of promises made by the government

Sample Plea Agreement Language

At the conclusion of defendant's cooperation, pursuant to this agreement, the United States will, at the time of sentencing, move pursuant to **Title 18, United States Code, Section 3553(e), Title 28, United States Code, Section 994(n) and Sentencing Guidelines §5K1.1** *that the court depart from the Guidelines and any applicable minimum sentence established by law to reflect defendant's substantial assistance in the investigation and prosecution. The United States will also bring the nature and extent of defendant's cooperation to the attention of the court, and the Bureau of Prisons, if applicable, at sentencing or any other appropriate time. The United States retains the right to make a sentencing recommendation, including a recommendation that the defendant receive a maximum possible sentence provided for under this agreement. The United States further retains the right to allocate at the time of sentencing. Defendant understands that the United States will bring to the attention of the court all pertinent facts concerning defendant's participation in any criminal activity, and all facts affecting the sentencing guidelines calculations.*

In a cooperation agreement, the government may makes several kinds of promises. Most importantly, the government may promise to make a motion for downward departure under USSG §5K1.1 for *substantial assistance*. Without this motion, there is no benefit to the defendant in most cases. Note that in order to permit departure below a statutory mandatory minimum, the government must also move for departure pursuant to 18 U.S.C. §3553(e). Melendez v. U.S., 518 U.S. 120 (1996) (government motion attesting to the defendant's substantial assistance in a criminal investigation and requesting that the district court depart below the minimum of the applicable *guideline sentencing range* does not also authorize the court to depart below a lower *statutory minimum sentence*). The government should also agree to bring the defendant's cooperation to the court's attention, including at least all of the criteria that USSG §5K1.1(a) lists as significant, such as truthfulness, completeness, reliability, nature and extent of assistance, injury or danger to defendant or his family, and timeliness. However, after the departure motions have been made by the government, downward departure by the court is discretionary, not mandatory. The appellate court has no jurisdiction to review the trial court's discretionary decision to refuse downward departure under **§5K1.1**. *U.S. v. Castellanos*, 904 F.2d 1490, 1497 (11th Cir.1990); *U.S. v. Vizcarra-Angulo*, 904 F.2d 22 (9th Cir.1990) (same); *U.S. v. Munoz*, 946 F.2d 729, 730-31 (10th Cir.1991) citing **U.S. v. Richardson**, 939 F.2d 135, 139-140 (4th Cir.1991) *cert. denied*, 502 U.S. 1061 (1992) (**§5K1.1** substantial assistance departure is discretionary); *U.S. v. Miro*, 29 F.3d 194 (5th Cir. 1994). *See also U.S. v. Hayes*, 939 F.2d 509, 511-13 (7th Cir.1991) (interpreting **18 U.S.C. §3553(e))**. Thus there appears to be no appellate relief if the defendant gets a §5K1.1 motion from the prosecution but the court refuses to depart. If, on the other hand, the government promises to make such a motion but fails to do so there may be relief under certain circumstances. *See* Section 3.7.9, below. The government may also reserve the right to make a *recommendation* based on the cooperation. Where possible this should be within a specific negotiated range. Or the government may agree to a *cap* under Rule **11(c)(1)(C)** something not done in the language above. This is always important, and may become more important if there is a breach of the agreement. If the plea is under **Rule 11(e)(1)(C)** (specific sentence) the judge must honor the agreement or allow the defendant to withdraw. *U.S. v. Fernandez*, 960 F.2d 771 (9th Cir. 1992).

Note that a provision like the one above saying that the government was free to provide all relevant information to the court at sentencing was held to override the protected nature of statements made during a proffer in plea negotiations, even though the proffer agreement itself provided that the information would not be used. *U.S. v. Fagge*, 101 F.3d 232 (2nd Cir. 1996) (discussed in Section 3.7.4). Under the same theory, namely that the plea agreement contract modifies any previous agreements, the government could possibly provide the court with information gained during cooperation under a promise of confidentiality.

3.7.6 Timing of sentencing proceedings

Sample Plea Agreement Language

The plea of guilty shall be entered as soon as practicable but the sentencing on the guilty plea will be deferred, with consent of the court, for a period of one year from the entry of the guilty plea, and upon motion of the government and concurrence of the court, for a period beyond that one year. It is the intention of the parties that sentencing on the instant charges be postponed until such time as defendant's cooperation and all related forfeiture actions have been completed.

The agreement provides that sentencing will be delayed for benefit of both parties. The government wants time for defendant to work, and the defendant wants more work to show the court. There should be an upper limit on the court's and the government's ability to delay the sentencing. Under this agreement, the court can refuse a continuance past one year and can force sentencing to go forward.

3.7.7 Determination of breach of agreement

Sample Plea Agreement Language

If there is a dispute regarding the obligations of the parties under this agreement, the United States District Court shall determine whether the United States or the defendant has failed to comply with this agreement including whether the defendant has been truthful.
Nothing shall limit the United States' methods of verifying the truthfulness of defendant's statements. As part of this process, in the sole discretion of the United States, the defendant agrees to submit to a polygraph examination to verify any information the defendant may provide to the United States, including but not limited to defendant's assets. Such examination will be conducted by a polygrapher chosen and conducted in a manner determined in the sole discretion of the United States. Neither party shall object to the admissibility in evidence of the results of such examination in any proceeding to enforce or set aside this agreement in which compliance with the terms of this agreement are in issue.

The usual breach in cooperation cases is failure to testify truthfully. The agreement provides that the court makes the final determination on failure to comply. Other forms of the agreement require the government to make a "good faith" determination on truthfulness, which may also lead to a hearing. The burden of proof on whether the agreement was breached is generally on the person alleging the breach. For example, before the government may decline to fulfill its obligations under a plea agreement, it must establish the defendant's breach by a preponderance of the evidence. See, e.g., *U.S. v. Crowell*, 997 F.2d 146, 148 (6th Cir.1993); *U.S. v. Tilley*, 964 F.2d 66, 71 (1st Cir.1992); *U.S. v. Verrusio*, 803 F.2d 885, 894 (7th Cir.1986). However, the burden can, in a sense, be reversed in a substantial assistance case. Where the defendant is claiming that the government breached the agreement by failing to move for assistance, the defendant may have to first demonstrate by a preponderance of the evidence that he provided the degree of assistance contemplated by the agreement. *U.S. v. Conner*, 930 F.2d 1073, 1076 (4th Cir. 1991). The sample agreement allows the government to require a polygraph exam. It does not condition the agreement on passing the exam, but it does make the exam admissible at a hearing on compliance. To counter this, the defense should try to insert an agreement that allows the defense to present its own polygraph evidence. In a case based on a similar agreement, the government introduced at trial a confession made by a cooperating defendant whose deal had fallen through after he failed a polygraph. The 9th Circuit originally showed its dislike of polygraphs by ruling that statements made in a cooperation deal conditioned on a polygraph were involuntary and could not be used after defendant failed the polygraph, describing the results of a polygraph as being out of the defendant's control and unreliable. *U.S. v. Escamilla*, 966 F.2d 465 (9th Cir. 1992) (withdrawn opinion). Unfortunately, that opinion was withdrawn and replaced with a narrower one that focused on the wording of the agreement, noting that the defendant had not specifically *agreed* that his confession would be admissible if he failed the polygraph. *U.S. v. Escamilla*, 975 F.2d 568 (9th Cir. 1992). Recently, the 9th Circuit has taken a more liberal, but still hostile, view of polygraphs under ***Daubert***. ***U.S. v. Cordova***, 104 F.3d 225 (9th Cir. 1997). ([W]e do not now hold that polygraph examinations are scientifically valid or that they will always assist the trier of fact ... We merely remove the obstacle of the per se rule against admissibility, which was based on antiquated concepts about the technical ability of the polygraph and legal precepts that have been expressly overruled by the Supreme Court.) See also ***U.S. v. Posado***, 57 F.3d 428, 431-34 (5th Cir.1995).

3.7.8 Penalties for breach by defendant

Sample Plea Agreement Language

If the defendant fails to comply with any obligation or promise pursuant to this agreement, the United States: 1) may, in its sole discretion, declare any provision of this agreement null and void in accordance with [the paragraph calling for the court to determine the breach] and the defendant understands that he/she will not be permitted to withdraw his/her plea of guilty made in connection with this agreement; 2) may indict and prosecute the defendant for any offense known to the United States for which he is responsible, including all offenses committed pursuant to his/her failure to cooperate, and defendant waives any statute of limitations, Speedy Trial Act and constitutional restrictions on bringing charges after the execution of this agreement; 3) may argue for a maximum sentence for the offenses to which defendant has plead guilty; 4) may use in any prosecution any information, statements, documents and evidence provided by defendant both before and after the plea agreement including derivative evidence; 5) may advise the Bureau of Prisons that defendant is no longer a cooperating witness, and recommend redesignation of defendant to a higher custodial level.

The agreement indicates that "any provision" may be declared null by the government, subject to review of the alleged breach by the court. The Double Jeopardy Clause does not prevent setting aside a plea and reinstating charges in the event of a breach. *Ricketts v. Adamson*, 483 U.S. 1, 9-10 (1987). But the government s remedies appear to be limited by several cases. For example, this part says that the defendant cannot withdraw her plea. However, if the plea is under **Rule 11(c)(1)(C)** (for a specific sentence) the judge must honor the agreement or allow the defendant to withdraw his plea. *U.S. v. Fernandez*, 960 F.2d 771 (9th Cir. 1992). It also says that the government can use any information provided by the defendant against the defendant. However, the 9th Circuit has prevented such use where the breach was failure to pass a polygraph, in the absence of a specific agreement to allow such use. *U.S. v. Escamilla*, 975 F.2d 568 (9th Cir. 1992). Nonetheless, the thrust of this part is clearly that all benefit will be lost in the event of a breach by defendant.

3.7.9 Remedies for breach by government

When the prosecution breaches a plea agreement, the breach may be remedied by either specific performance of the agreement or by allowing the defendant to withdraw the plea. *U.S. v. Skidmore*, 998 F.2d 372, 375 (6th Cir. 1993). Where the government agrees to file a **§5K1.1** motion *if* the defendant provides substantial assistance, the government s failure to file after determining that the assistance was not substantial is not a breach. *U.S. v. Price*, 95 F.3d 364 (5th Cir. 1996); *U.S. v. Knight*, 96 F.3d 307 (8th Cir. 1996), Such refusals are reviewed by the district court only on a limited basis, to determine if the refusal was arbitrary or was based on an unconstitutional motive (*e.g.*, racial discrimination). Wade v. U.S., 504 U.S. 181 (1992). *See* ***U.S. v. King***, 62 F.3d 891, 894, n.2 (7th Cir. 1995) (refusing to review failure to make motion, but noting that a few courts say it may be reviewable if irrational or withheld in bad faith). *See also* ***U.S. v. De la Fuente***, 8 F.3d 1333 (9th Cir. 1993) (motion to depart from statutory minimum could not be withheld where to do so would imply bad faith on the part of the government because defendant would receive no benefit for his cooperation); ***U.S. v. Moore***, 225 F.3d 637, 641 (6th Cir. 2000) (court may only review the government s decision for unconstitutional motives).

Where the government agrees to recommend a reduction if the defendant is truthful when debriefed by agents, the government s failure to debrief the defendant prior to his sentencing is a breach of the agreement, particularly where the debriefing could have allowed the defendant to satisfy the one remaining requirement he needed for safety valve protection. ***U.S. v. Beltran-Ortiz***, 91 F.3d 665 (4th Cir. 1996). The government s agreement to move for 5K1.1 departure if the defendant provided substantial assistance obligated the government to give the defendant the *opportunity* to furnish such assistance. ***U.S. v. Laday***, 56 F.3d 24 (5th Cir. 1995).

Although defendant changed his plea to nolo contendere and was denying knowledge of much of the criminal activity, the government knew that when it amended the plea agreement to allow the nolo plea. The amended agreement still included the substantial assistance provision and thus the government was obligated to carry through and allow defendant to try to cooperate Where government agreed to present a Rule 35 motion detailing extent of defendants post-sentence cooperation, but details of the cooperation were not in the motion for security reasons and the court refused to grant an evidentiary hearing on the motion, the government was effectively prevented from presenting the Rule 35 motion and the plea agreement was breached. *U.S. v. Hernandez*, 34 F.3d 998 (11th Cir. 1994) (case came up on appeal from the denial of the **Rule 35** motion and the appellate court vacated and remanded for an evidentiary hearing).

3.8 Agreements Regarding Deportation

A fast track policy allowing illegal re-entry defendants to stipulate to a two year sentence and waive appeal under *8 U.S.C. § 1326(a)* (simple reentry after deportation), in order to avoid 1326(b) (reentry after deportation with felony conviction), showed no discriminatory intent and passed constitutional muster. *U.S. v. Estrada-Plata,* 57 F.3d 757 (9th Cir.1995). **(see also, Section 6.2, below)**

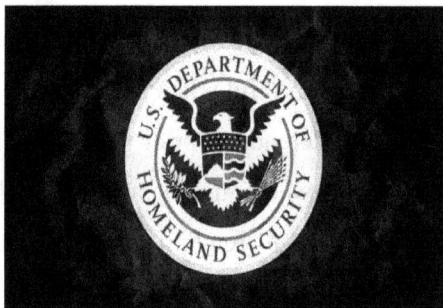

Waivers: Trial, Brady, Appeal, and Collateral

The waiver section of a plea agreement usually covers two distinct types of waivers. First, there is the set of non-negotiable waivers that must accompany any guilty plea, such as the waiver of the right to trial. Second, there is the somewhat more negotiable set of waivers that the prosecution tries to extract in return for the plea bargain, such as the waiver of the right to appeal.

4.1 Waiver of Trial and Attendant Rights

The general waiver sections of plea agreements vary from minimal to extensive. A few sample paragraphs from a fairly long waiver section are set out below.

Sample Plea Agreement Language

Advice by attorney: *I have read each of the provisions of the plea agreement with assistance of counsel and I understand it. I have discussed the case and my constitutional and other rights with my attorney. I have been advised by my attorney of the nature of the charge[s], of the nature and range of the possible sentence, and that my ultimate sentence will be determined according to the guidelines promulgated pursuant to the Sentencing Reform Act of 1984. I am satisfied that my defense attorney has represented me in a competent manner.*

Waiver of trial rights: *I understand that by entering my plea of guilty I will be giving up my rights to plead not guilty, to trial by jury, to confront, cross-examine, and compel the attendance of witnesses, to present evidence in my defense, to remain silent and refuse to be a witness against myself by asserting my privilege against self-incrimination all with the assistance of counsel and to be presumed innocent until proven guilty beyond a reasonable doubt.*

Acting on own volition with clear mind: *My guilty plea is not the result of force, threats, assurances or promises other than the promises contained in this agreement. I agree to the* *provisions of this agreement as a voluntary act on my part, rather than at the direction of or because of the recommendation of any other person, and I agree to be bound according to its provisions. I am not now on or under the influence of any drug, medication, liquor, or other intoxicant or depressant, which would impair my ability to fully understand the terms and conditions of this plea agreement.*

Merger clause: *I agree that this written plea agreement contains all the terms and conditions of my plea and that promises made by anyone (including my attorney), and specifically any predictions as to the guideline range applicable, that are not contained within this written plea agreement are without force and effect and are null and void.*

Rule 11(b), FRCrP, lays out a laundry list of things of which the court must advise the defendant, including information about penalties that could be imposed, the right to representation (at no cost if needed), the right to go to trial and attendant rights, the effect of a plea of guilty on those rights, and a warning about testifying under oath. Case law identifies notice of three particular rights as constitutionally essential the right to confront accusers, the right to a trial by jury, and the privilege against compulsory self-incrimination. ***Boykin v. Alabama***, 395 U.S. 238 (1969). The catch-all provision above covers those Rule 11 and Boykin rights not covered elsewhere in a typical agreement. Some attorneys dislike the reference to their competency, but the defendant will often be asked that question by the judge in one form or another during the colloquy anyway.

This agreement waives many of the rights attendant on trial. Some plea agreements go farther and contain a waiver of sentencing rights, such as the right to seek a downward departure. Although such waivers have become common in immigration cases, it is also beginning to appear in other types of cases.

4.2 Waiver of Brady Material Pre-Plea

The government can require a defendant to waive her Brady right to disclosure of impeachment evidence as a condition of a plea agreement. *U.S. v. Ruiz* , 536 U.S. 622 (2002). In Ruiz, defendant refused to accept a "fast track" plea bargain, under which government would recommend downward departure under Sentencing Guidelines if she pleaded guilty, because it contained waiver of Brady right to disclosure of impeachment evidence. Defendant ultimately entered a guilty plea without an agreement, then appealed, challenging the government's refusal to recommend, and court's refusal to grant, downward departure. Note the odd procedural posture: Ruiz actually refused to enter into a plea agreement, pled straight up, then complained that her plea was involuntary because she would have entered in to the agreement (and reduced her sentence) if the government had not unconstitutionally refused to proceed without a *Brady* waiver. Nonetheless, the Supreme Court treated this as an issue of the voluntariness of the plea and held that (1) the Constitution does not require government to disclose impeachment information prior to entering plea agreement with criminal defendant; and (2) plea agreement requiring defendant to waive her right to receive information the government had regarding any "affirmative defense" she would raise at trial did not violate the Constitution. As to both types of information, the court held that the Constitution did not require them to be provided to the defendant prior to plea bargaining primarily because the need for this information is more closely related to the *fairness of a trial* than to the *voluntariness of the plea*. ***U.S. v. Ruiz*** , 536 U.S. 622, 632 (2002). Disclosure of some Brady material may still be required prior to a plea. The Seventh Circuit stated that the Supreme Court has yet to address, however, whether the Due Process Clause requires [***Brady***] disclosures outside the context of a trial and that Ruiz actually indicates that such a claim might be viable in certain cases. ***McCann v. Mangialardi***, 337 F.3d 782, 787 (7th Cir. 2003). The analysis is interesting: In holding that the Due Process Clause does not require the government to disclose impeachment information prior to the entry of a criminal defendant's guilty plea, the Court in Ruiz reasoned that it was "particularly difficult to characterize impeachment information as critical information of which the defendant must always be aware prior to pleading guilty ...." 536 U.S. at 630, 122 S.Ct. 2450 (emphasis added). The Court also noted that "the proposed plea agreement at issue ... specifies the Government will provide 'any information establishing the factual innocence of the defendant,' " id. at 631, 122 S.Ct. 2450, and "[t]hat fact, along with other guilty-plea safeguards ... diminishes the force of [defendant's] concern that, in the absence of the impeachment information, innocent individuals accused of crimes will plead guilty." Id. Thus, Ruiz indicates a significant distinction between impeachment information and exculpatory evidence of actual innocence. Given this distinction, it is highly likely that the Supreme Court would find a violation of the Due Process Clause if prosecutors or other relevant government actors have knowledge of a criminal defendant's factual innocence but fail to disclose such information to a defendant before he enters into a guilty plea. *Id* at 787-788 (emphasis added). Courts have not all treated Ruiz as a blanket approval for all kinds of missing information prior to a plea. For example, the Ninth Circuit held that Ruiz did not prevent relief where the defendant was misled to believe that drug quantity needed to be proved only by a preponderance of the evidence, holding that the true burden of proof goes directly to the nature of the charge against Villalobos and to the voluntariness of his plea, and is properly characterized as critical information of which the defendant must always be aware prior to pleading guilty. **U.S. v. Villalobos**, 333 F.3d 1070, 1075 n. 6 (9th Cir. 2003).

4.3 Waiver of Appeal

Waiver of appeal is a fairly recent development. More and more it is becoming a non-negotiable part of the agreement. Appellate courts generally favor the waiver. A sample appeal waiver follows:

Sample Plea Agreement Language

> *Defendant hereby waives any right to raise and/or appeal any and all motions, defenses, probable cause determinations, and objections which defendant has asserted or could assert to this prosecution and to the court's entry of judgment against defendant and imposition of sentence upon defendant consistent with this agreement. Defendant further waives any right to appeal this Court's imposition of sentence upon him under* **Title 18, United States Code, Section 3742** *(sentence appeals).*

4.3.1 Statutory limits on right to appeal.

Although defendants who plead not guilty have a right to appeal their conviction including rulings on such things as pretrial motions under **Rule**

32(j)(1)(A), FRCrP, a defendant who pleads guilty has only a limited right to appeal a sentence under **Rule 32(j)(1)(B), FRCrP,** and *18 U.S.C. 3742(a).* Defendants may appeal when the sentence (1) violates law, (2) is based on incorrect guideline application, (3) is greater than the guidelines allow, or (4) is for a crime that has no guideline and is plainly unreasonable. Further restrictions that apply in the case of a plea agreement under **Rule 11(c)(1)(C)** stipulated sentence are set out in *18 U.S.C. 3742(c)(1).* Generally, appeals under parts (3) and (4) above sentence above guidelines or sentence unreasonable and no guideline are not permitted if the stipulated sentence is not exceeded.

4.3.2 Conditional Pleas

With the consent of the court and the government, a defendant may plead guilty and reserve in writing the right to appeal an adverse determination of a specified pretrial motion. **Rule 11(a)(2)**, FRCrP. A conditional guilty plea carries with it the special requirement that it be in writing so that a precise record can be made both of the fact of the government s consent and the specified pretrial motion, **Rule 11(a)(2)**, which the defendant reserves the right to challenge. *U.S. v. Herrera*, 265 F.3d 349, 351 (6th Cir. 2001) The rule places an affirmative duty on the defendant to preserve any issues collateral to the determination of guilt or innocence by specifying them in the plea itself. *U.S. v. Ormsby*, 252 F.3d 844, 848 (6th Cir. 2001)

4.3.3 Defense waivers of appeal rights are generally effective.

In general, an express waiver of the right to appeal in a negotiated plea agreement is valid. *U.S. v. Schmidt*, 47 F.3d 188 (7th Cir.1995) citing *U.S. v. Bushert*, 997 F.2d 1343, 1347-50 (11th Cir..1993), *cert. denied*, 513 U.S. 1051 (1994); *U.S. v. Melancon*, 972 F.2d 566, 567-68 (5th Cir.1992); *U.S. v. Rivera*, 971 F.2d 876, 896 (2d Cir.1992); *U.S. v. Rutan*, 956 F.2d 827, 829 (8th Cir.1992); *U.S. v. Navarro-Botello,* 912 F.2d 318, 321-22 (9th Cir.1990**), cert. denied**, 503 U.S. 942, 112 S.Ct. 1488, 117 35 L.Ed.2d 629 (1992); *U.S. v. Wiggins*, 905 F.2d 51, 52-54 (4th Cir.1990); *see also U.S. v. Hendrickson*, 22 F.3d 170, 174 (7th Cir...1994), *cert. denied*, 513 U.S. 898 (1994) (finding no waiver of the right to appeal because such a waiver "must be express and unambiguous"); *Griffen v. U.S.,* 109 F.3d 1217 (7th Cir. 1997) (permitting a habeas action to proceed on issue of whether waiver was the result of ineffective assistance of counsel). The remedy for an invalid waiver clause is severance of the clause, not invalidation of the plea. Thus the defendant can appeal, but the plea and sentence remain in effect unless the appeal is successful. *U.S. v. Bushert*, 997 F.2d 1343, 1350-54 (11th Cir...1993), *cert. denied*, 513 U.S. 1051 (1994).

4.3.4 Appeal waivers must be knowing and voluntary

A waiver of appeal must be knowing and voluntary. *U.S. v. Bushert*, 997 F.2d 1343, 1350-54 (11th Cir.1993), *cert. denied*, 513 U.S. 1051 (1994). A waiver is knowing if the court advises defendant of the waiver or if it is manifestly clear that defendant understood the full significance of waiver. *Id.*; *U.S. v. Marin*, 961 F.2d 493, 496 (4th Cir..1992). *See also*

U.S. v. Benitez-Zapata, 131 F.3d 1444 (11th Cir. 1997) (holding that waiver will be upheld if either: (1) the district court specifically questioned the defendant about the waiver during the colloquy, or (2) the record clearly shows that the defendant understood the full significance of the waiver). The 5th Circuit has upheld a waiver in a written plea agreement even where the court did not advise the defendant of the waiver, in the absence of any indication that the defendant did not understand it. *U.S. v. Portillo*, 18 F.2d 290, (5th Cir. 1994), *cert. denied*, 513 U.S.893 (1994); *Accord*, *U.S. v. Michelsen*, 141 f3d 868 (8th Cir. 1998). See *U.S. v. Agee*, 83 F.3d 882 (7th Cir. 1996) (specific dialogue with defendant not needed); *U.S. v. Michlin*, 34 F.3d 896, 898 (9th Cir.1994) (waiver good even though court did not specifically advise defendant of waiver provision). On the other hand, a waiver was struck down where the colloquy indicated that the defendant did not really understand it even though it was in the written agreement. *U.S. v. Baty*, 980 F.2d 977 (5th Cir. 1992), *cert. denied*, 508 U.S. 956 (1993). The 11th Circuit has held that, unless there is a manifestly clear indication in the record that the defendant understood the full significance of his appeal waiver, a lack of sufficient inquiry by the district court during the Rule 11 hearing would be error and would invalidate the appeal waiver. *U.S. v. Bushert*, 997 F.2d 1343, 1352 (11th Cir. 1993), *cert. denied*, 513

66

U.S. 1051 (1994). The 9th Circuit rejects this argument, saying that a Rule 11 colloquy on the waiver of appeal is not necessary, and that a finding that the waiver is knowing and voluntary can be based on the text of the plea agreement, the fact that the waiver is mentioned in the presentence report, and the presumption that the lawyer has discussed both of these with the defendant. *U.S. v. DeSantiago-Martinez*, 38 F.3d 394, 395 (9th Cir. 1992), *cert. denied*, 513 U.S. 1128 (1995).

Note that if the court advises a defendant that he *has* a right to appeal, that may override a waiver in the plea agreement, *U.S. v. Buchanan*, 59 F.3d 914, 917 (9th Cir. 1996), unless the district court s advice indicated some doubt about the right to appeal. *U.S. v. Martinez*, 143 F.3d 1266, 1272 (9th Cir. 1998). *But see U.S. v. Michelsen*, 141 F.3d 867 (8th Cir. 1998) (where advice of right to appeal came at time of sentencing, it was irrelevant to the earlier decision to plead). The result may be different if the prosecutor makes a timely objection to the court s advice, even if the court refuses to change it. There is also a possibility of implicit waiver of a defendant s appeal rights as to certain issues. Courts have held in numerous cases that a *defendant* waives any objection that he fails to make in the district court. See, e.g., *U.S. v. Belden*, 957 F.2d 671 (9th Cir. 1992), *cert. denied*, 506 U.S. 882 (1992).

4.3.5 Some appeal waivers may be invalid

A jurisdictional challenge based on a defective indictment is not waived by the waiver of the right to appeal in a plea agreement. *U.S. v. Ruelas*, 106 F.3d 1416 (9th Cir. 1997), Nor will a waiver prevent an appeal "where the sentence imposed is not in accordance with the negotiated agreement". *Navarro-Botello*, *supra* at 321. If the sentence is outside the agreed range, the waiver clause is void and defendant can appeal all aspects of the sentence, even those that did not violate plea agreement. **U.S. v. Haggard**, 41 F.3d 1320, 1325 (9th Cir..1994). On the other hand, where the sentence does not exceed an agreed cap, waiver is effective even though the sentence exceeds the guidelines and is not adequately justified as a departure. *U.S. v. Bollinger*, 940 F.2d 478 (9th Cir. 1991). Thus, at least in the 9th Circuit, any agreement to a cap, in combination with a waiver, gives the court license to disregard the guidelines as long as it honors the cap. Appeal in spite of a waiver was allowed in *U.S. v. Kelly*, 974 F.2d 22 (5th Cir. 1992), where the term of supervised release exceeded the statutory maximum. *See also U.S. v. Bushert*, 997 F.2d 1343, 1350-54 (11th Cir.1993) (waiver not applicable if sentence is in excess of maximum penalty provided by statute or violates equal protection or violates plea agreement). *See also U.S. v. Broughton-Jones*, 71 F.3d 1143, 1147 (4th Cir. 1995) (allowing appeal despite waiver where defendant claimed that restitution exceeded the amount allowed by statute, making this similar to a claim of a sentence above the statutory maximum*); U.S. v. Zink*, 107 F.3d 716 (9th Cir. 1997) (following *U.S. v. Catherine*, 55 F.3d 1462 (9th Cir. 1995) and *U.S. v. Ready*, 82 F.3d 551 (2d Cir. 1996)) (defendant who waives his right to appeal a sentence may not have waived his right to appeal restitution, where the plea agreement had specific references to guidelines and maximum sentences but no references to restitution, and restitution was outside the guidelines but note that the court also *told* Zink he could appeal, which may have had some effect on the decision). Waiver of appeal may be subject to certain exceptions such as claims of breach of the plea agreement, racial disparity in sentencing among co-defendants, or illegal sentence in excess of the statutory maximum. *U.S. v. Baramdyka*, 95 F.3d 840 (9th Cir. 1996), 117 S.Ct. 1282 (1997). *Baramdyka* was cited in *U.S. v. Martinez*, 143 F.3d 1266, 1270-71 (9th Cir. 1998) for the proposition that a waiver is generally enforceable if the language of the waiver encompasses the defendant s right to appeal on the grounds claimed on appeal . This is reasonable, but somewhat circular. Appeal may also be allowed where the violation of rights appealed from occurs *after* the waiver, as where a defendant was arguably denied counsel at sentencing after attorney withdrew. *U.S. v. Attar*, 38 F.3d 727, 732 (4th Cir. 1994). It appears to be difficult for the government to waive the defendant s waiver . In one case, the government did not raise the issue of defendant's waiver in its brief to the appellate court. The court noticed the clause *sua sponte*, found it to be valid, and declined to reach the merits of defendant's argument. *U.S. v. Schmidt*, 47 F.3d 188, 190 (7th Cir.1995). The dissent suggested that if the government chose not to argue that defendant has waived appeal rights, this decision (to waive the waiver clause) should be respected by the court. *Id.*, (Ripple, J. in dissent). *See also U.S. v. Doe*, 53 F.3d 1081, 1082-83 (9th Cir. 1995) (noting general rule that court will not address waiver if not raised by the opposing party albeit in a case where the government urged the court to reach the merits).

4.3.6 Government waiver of appeal rights

The 11th Circuit has found an implicit waiver of the right to appeal where the prosecutor agreed that the court had discretion and did not object to downward departure. *U.S. v. Prickett*, 898 F.2d 130 (11th Cir. 1990).

However, the 9th Circuit has found an exception to allow the government to appeal where there was plain error and "injustice". *U.S. v. Snider*, 957 F.2d 703 (9th Cir. 1992). The government could also be prevented from appealing certain types of errors if the sentence is not less than the agreed "specific sentence". *18 U.S.C. §3742(c)(2).*

4.4 Waiver of Collateral Review

Sample Plea Agreement Language

> *Further, defendant hereby waives any right to raise, appeal, and/or file any post-conviction writs of habeas corpus or **coram nobis** concerning any and all motions, defenses, hearings, probable cause determinations, and objections which defendant has asserted or could assert to this prosecution or to the court's entry of judgment against defendant and imposition of sentence upon defendant consistent with this agreement.*

In addition to waiving direct appeal, the provision above purports to waive any kind of post conviction relief such as writ of habeas corpus. This may create an ethical problem, as the attorney who is advising the client to enter into the guilty plea is probably the same attorney that the client would be calling ineffective counsel in a post-conviction action. Can that attorney ethically advise the client to waive the potential claim against the attorney? Some bar associations have issued advisory ethics opinions on this issue, but the situation is not clear. In the wake of those opinions, some defenders have sought opinions on the same subject from their state bar committees. The 5th Circuit has upheld waivers of collateral relief. *U.S. v.*

Wilkes, 20 F.3d 651 (5th Cir. 1994). However, waiver of appeal does not include waiver of ineffective assistance of counsel claim under **21 U.S.C. § 2255**. *U.S. v. Pruitt*, 32 F.3d 431, 433 (9th Cir. 1994). Dismissal of an appeal on waiver grounds would be inappropriate where defendant files a motion to withdraw from the plea because the waiver was tainted by ineffective assistance of counsel. *U.S. v. Price*, 95 F.3d 364, 369 (5th Cir. 1996) (although Price appeal was dismissed because he did *not* file a motion to withdraw). The 9th Circuit also has faced the problem of counsel advising a defendant to waive claims of ineffective assistance of counsel, although in a slightly different form. In *U.S. v. Muro*, 87 F.3d 1078 (9th Cir. 1996), the defendant claimed that his counsel was ineffective and asked that a new one be appointed to argue his motion for new trial on that ground. The district court refused and forced the ineffective counsel to handle the evidentiary hearing on the motion. The 9th Circuit reversed, stating that forcing a lawyer to try to prove his own ineffectiveness at an evidentiary hearing for new trial created an inherent conflict of interest. The same type of conflict analysis should apply to waiving the right to make ineffective assistance claims.

4.5 Conditional Waivers

A conditional waiver of appeal was enforced in *U.S. v. Littlefield*, 105 F.3d 527(9th Cir. 1997). Littlefield s waiver was conditional upon the sentence being within the agreed cap. It was, so he could not appeal.

5 Miscellaneous Typical Provisions

5.1 PENALTIES

The penalties section of a plea agreement sets forth the maximum penalties that the law allows for the charge to which the defendant will plead. Its only real functions are to make sure that the defendant has been properly advised of the penalties and to inform the judge of what to tell the defendant at the change of plea hearing.

Sample Plea Agreement Language

*a) A violation of **Title 21 U.S.C. §841(a)(1)** and **§841(b)(1)(A)(vii)**, is punishable by a mandatory minimum term of imprisonment of ten years, and a maximum term of imprisonment of up to life, or a maximum fine of $4,000,000 or both.*

b) According to the Sentencing Guidelines, the court shall:

*1) Order the defendant to make restitution to any victim of the offense, unless, pursuant to **Title 18, U.S.C. §3663**, the court determines that restitution would not be appropriate;*

*2) Order the defendant to pay a fine, unless, pursuant **to Section 5E1.2(f)** of the Guidelines, the defendant establishes the applicability of the exceptions found therein;*

*3) Order the defendant, pursuant to **Title 18 U.S.C. §3583** to serve a term of supervised   release when required by law or when a sentence of imprisonment of more than one year is imposed, the court may impose a term of supervised released in all other cases.*

*c) Pursuant to **Title 18 U.S.C. §§3561-3566, §3559**, the defendant may not be sentenced   to a period of probation.*

d) Pursuant to Title 18 §3013, the court is required to impose a special assessment on the defendant of $100.00 per count.

5.1.1 Common errors in penalty terms

Maximum incarceration terms are usually correct, as they are set out in the statutes. Mandatory minimum terms must be checked carefully, particularly in drug, gun and Continuing Criminal Enterprise (CCE) cases. Authorized supervised release terms are often wrong. They are controlled in general by *18 U.S.C. §3583,* which in turn relies on the classification of the offense under *18 U.S.C. §3559*. Specific statutes sometimes have their own supervised release requirements, such as the drug statute *21 U.S.C. §841*. Authorized fines amounts are often wrong. Fines for offenses before the guidelines went into effect are controlled by the specific statute. Guideline case fines are controlled by the greater of the specific statute or the fine in *18 U.S.C. §3571*, which was amended in December of 1987 to change the misdemeanor fines. The general fine statute relies on the classification of the offense under *18 U.S.C. §3559*. Special assessments are controlled by 18 U.S.C. §3013, which provides for smaller assessments for class A, B, and C misdemeanors. The section was amended in 1996 to provide for $100, as opposed to $50, assessments for felonies.

5.1.2 Effect of errors in penalty terms

Rule 11(c)(1) requires that defendants be advised of the mandatory minimum provided by law, if any, and the maximum possible penalty including the effect of special parole or supervised release. Many mistakes in advising defendants are harmless errors, generally because the defendant receives a sentence well below the maximum. *U.S. v. Sanclemente-Bejarano*, 861 F.2d 206, 209-10 (9th Cir. 1988) (harmless error where defendant was advised maximum sentence was life imprisonment and received 15 years sentence and five year term of supervised release). However, there may be harmful error where the combination of sentences received could cause defendant s liberty to be restricted beyond the maximum sentences described. *See U.S. v. Roberts*, 5 F.3d 365 (9th Cir. 1993) (defendant was not advised of supervised release and receive maximum term and maximum supervised release). Also, advising a

defendant that he was subject to a five year mandatory minimum at arraignment, and then finding him responsible for more cocaine at sentencing, triggering a mandatory 10 year sentence, invalidated his guilty plea. *U.S. v. Still*, 102 F.3d 118 (5th Cir., 1996), *cert. denied*, 118 S.Ct. 43 (1997). Failure to mention restitution during plea colloquy was harmless error, where defendant was made aware of the restitution obligation through his plea and cooperation agreements. *U.S. v. McCarty*, 99 F.3d 383 (11th Cir. 1996). It was also harmless error where defendant was advised of a possible fine but not of possible restitution and the restitution imposed was less than the fine could have been. U.S. v. Pomazi, 851 F.2d 244 (9th Cir. 1998), *overruled in part on other grounds*, *Hughey v. U.S.*, 495 U.S. 411 (1990). It has been suggested that now that restitution is mandatory under the MVRA failure to advise of restitution runs afoul of the **Rule 11(c)(1)** requirement that mandatory minimums be mentioned. *See* Section 3.6.3.

The remedy in some cases for a bad penalty advisement has been a direction by the appellate court that the district court vacate the part of the sentence that exceeds the advisement, rather than allowing the defendant to withdraw his plea. *U.S. v. Rogers*, 984 F.2d 314 (9th Cir. 1993).

There may also be error where it appears that the decision to plead was impacted by the erroneous advice given by the court. For example, in a situation where a defendant was told at arraignment that he faced 60 years for two drug counts but he actually faced only 30 years, where he pled guilty to one or the counts in return for dismissal of the other, and where the court thought he was subject to 30 years which he was not and sentenced him to 15, the defendant s guilty plea and waiver of trial was invalid. *U.S. v. Guerra*, 94 F.3d 989 (5th Cir. 1996) (significantly, there was nothing in the record suggesting that defendant ever received the correct information about his exposure from his counsel).

Note that it is also possible that failure of the attorney to advise the defendant of certain consequences of the plea, such as failure to warn of possible career offender status, may be ineffective assistance of counsel. *Risher v. U.S.*, 992 F.2d 982 (9th Cir. 1993).

5.2 Warnings

The warnings are usually spread around in the plea agreement, but have been grouped here for discussion.

5.2.1 Perjury and other false statement offenses

Sample Plea Agreement Language

Nothing in this agreement shall be construed to protect the defendant in any way from   prosecution for perjury, false declaration or false statement, as defined by the law of any sovereign, or any other offense committed by defendant after the date of this agreement. Any information, statements, documents, and evidence which defendant provides to the   United States pursuant to this agreement may be used against him in any such prosecutions.

This paragraph makes explicit the policy set out in **USSG §1B1.8(b)(3)** regarding the use of information provided in cooperation agreements in a later perjury prosecution.

5.2.2 Reinstitution of prosecution

Sample Plea Agreement Language

If defendant's guilty plea is rejected, withdrawn, vacated, or reversed at any time, the United States will be free to prosecute the defendant for all charges of which it has knowledge, and any charges that have been dismissed because of this plea agreement will be automatically reinstated. In such event, defendant waives any objections, motions, or defenses based upon the Statute of Limitations, the Speedy Trial Act or constitutional restrictions on bringing of charges.

This is the government side of the back to square one provision. Because under some circumstance a defendant may be able to withdraw from a plea or have a plea set aside on appeal, the government wants to be able to get back to the *status quo ante* in that event. This kind of provision is not unfair, but is very hard to explain to poorly educated or non-English speaking clients. The second sentence in the above sample language is probably overly broad. It should only waive impediments to prosecution that have resulted from the delay caused by the plea proceedings. No case has surfaced where this language has been used for any more nefarious purpose.

5.2.3 Disclosure of information to Probation Office and Court

Sample Plea Agreement Language

Defendant understands the United States' obligation to provide all information in its file regarding defendant, including charged and uncharged criminal offenses, to the United States Probation Office.

This provision describes, and perhaps causes, a problem. The probation office gets the information on all the conduct known to the prosecutor even if the defendant only pleads to part of it. This is the genesis of the problems regarding consideration of dismissed and uncharged conduct, because it requires the prosecution to give the probation officer information on such conduct which the officer then uses to increase the defendant s guidelines.

Note that a similar provision in a plea agreement saying that the government was free to provide all relevant information to the court at sentencing was held to override the protected nature of statements made during a proffer in plea negotiations, even though proffer agreement itself provided that the information would not be used, . *U.S. v. Fagge*, 101 F.3d 232 (2nd Cir. 1996) (discussed in Section 3.7.4). At sentencing the judge asked the government why the defendant was not entitled to a minimal role adjustment and the government used information from the proffers to show that defendant had engaged in several drug deals. The court of appeals held that the language in the plea agreement overrode the proffer agreement. This provision raises new concerns in the post-*Booker* world, as discussed above in section 3.7.4.

5.2.4 Effect on forfeiture, civil, and administrative proceedings

Sample Plea Agreement Language

Nothing in this agreement shall be construed to protect the defendant from civil forfeiture proceedings or prohibit the United States from proceeding with and/or initiating an action for civil forfeiture. Further, this agreement does not preclude the United States from instituting any civil or administrative proceedings as may be appropriate now or in the future.

This provision reflects the government s concern that the Double Jeopardy Clause may be implicated when a defendant receives a sentence in one proceeding and suffers a civil forfeiture in another. The Supreme Court found that a tax on marijuana imposed on the defendant after the defendant was prosecuted for possession of the marijuana constituted a violation of double jeopardy. ***Montana Department of Revenue v. Kurth Ranch***, 511 U.S. 767 (1994). The tax was authorized by the same statute as the prosecution and was conditioned upon the commission of the crime. Prior to ***Kurth Ranch***, the Supreme Court had also upheld the double jeopardy complaint where what was denominated a civil penalty was imposed after a conviction, but the court found that the penalty was non-remedial and had a punitive character. ***U.S. v. Halper***, 490 U.S. 435 (1989). Taken together these cases had fairly put an end to the practice of following criminal convictions with civil forfeiture actions. In most cases, the government began to seek forfeiture *in* the criminal action, thus avoiding the bar.

However, the Supreme Court in ***U.S. v. Ursery***, 518 U.S. 267 (1996), recently held that *in rem* civil forfeitures are neither punishment nor criminal and thus do not create a double jeopardy problem. *See also* ***Hudson v. U.S.***, 522 U.S. 93, 118 S.Ct. 488 (1997) (no bar to prosecution for misapplication of bank funds where defendant already suffered monetary penalties and occupational debarment at hands of Comptroller of Currency largely disavowing the Harper analysis and finding the previous penalties to be civil remedies).

5.3 Factual Basis

The factual basis section establishes that there are sufficient facts to support a conviction. These facts may also form the basis of some of the probation officer s guideline calculations and must be examined carefully. **Rule 11(b)(3)** requires the court to determine that there is a factual basis for the plea.

Sample Plea Agreement Language

I further agree that if this matter were to proceed to trial the United States could prove the following facts beyond a reasonable doubt, and that these facts accurately represent my readily provable offense conduct and specific offense characteristics: [facts of the offense of conviction]

As mentioned in other sections, the guidelines provide that stipulation to a greater offense may require the use of the guideline for that offense. USSG §1B1.2(a). Under the revised comment to **USSG §1B1.2**, however, the defendant must explicitly agree that a factual statement or stipulation will have that effect. If that condition is met, then if the defendant pled guilty to one offense but stipulated to a more serious offense in the factual basis, the court will sentence the defendant based on the guideline for the more serious offense. *U.S. v. Martin*, 893 F.2d 73, 74-76 (5th Cir.1990);

see also ***U.S. v. Gardner***, 940 F.2d 587, 590-92 (10th Cir. 1991) (defendant pled guilty to bank larceny, stipulated to bank robbery, sentenced for bank robbery). Inadequacy of factual basis is waived where at sentencing defendant failed to raise the issue and defense counsel agreed that a basis existed. ***U.S. v. Reyes-Alvarado***, 963 F.2d 1184 (9th Cir. 1992).

5.4 Approval and Acceptance

5.4.1 DEFENSE ATTORNEY APPROVAL

The defense attorney approval section, requiring counsel s signature rather than the defendant s, basically tries to lock defense counsel in to vouch for the plea.

Sample Plea Agreement Language

*I have discussed this case and the plea agreement with my client in detail and have advised the defendant in all matters within the scope of **Fed.R.Crim.P. 11**, the constitutional and other rights of an accused, the factual basis for and the nature of the offense to which the guilty plea will be entered, possible defenses, and the consequences of the guilty plea. No assurances, promises, or representations have been given to me or to the defendant by the United States or by any of its representatives which are not contained in this written agreement. I concur in the entry of the plea as indicated above and on the terms and conditions set forth in this agreement as in the best interests of my client. I agree to make a bona fide effort to ensure that the guilty plea is entered in accordance with all the requirements of **Fed.R.Crim.P. 11**.*

Failure to properly advise the defendant of the elements of the offense, defenses, or penalties, resulting in a mistaken decision to plead guilty, has always been possible ineffective assistance of counsel. Now failure to properly advise defendant on sentencing guidelines, resulting in a defendant's decision *not* to take a plea bargain, can also be ineffective assistance. *U.S. v. Day*, 969 F.2d 39 (3rd Cir. 1992); *U.S. v. Sanders*, 3 F.Supp. 2d 554 (M.D.Penn 1998). Failure to warn a client of possible career offender status has also been held to be ineffective assistance. *Risher v. U.S.*, 992 F.2d 982 (1993).

The remedy for such a failures is not completely clear. *In re Alvernaz*, 2 Cal. Rptr. 2nd 713, 830 P.2d 747 (Cal. Sup. Ct. 1992) suggests that where a defendant failed to accept a plea bargain because of ineffective counsel, the remedy would be modification of the judgment consistent with the plea offer or a new trial with resumption of the plea negotiation process. When the same case came before a federal district court on a habeas claim, the court ordered that Alvarnaz be allowed to consider the former offer with assistance of competent counsel. *Alvernaz v. Ratelle*, 831 F.Supp 790 (S.D.Cal. 1993). Where a plea offer was never communicated to the client, the 9th Circuit has said that the remedy would be reinstatement of the plea offer. *U.S. v. Blaylock*, 20 F.3d 1458 (9th Cir. 1994). To be eligible for relief, the defendant has to demonstrate that he would have accepted the plea had it been communicated. *Engelen v. U.S.*, 68 F.3d 238 (8th Cir. 1995) (citing *Blaylock*).

5.4.2 Government approval

Sample Plea Agreement Language

I have reviewed this matter and the plea agreement. I agree on behalf of the United States that the terms and conditions set forth are appropriate and are in the best interests   of justice.

The government approval section is usually nothing more than a signature block, and has no real significance beyond making the government a party to the contract .

5.4.3 Court acceptance

Rule 11(e)(2) *allows* the court to delay acceptance of the plea agreement until after the presentence report in the case of a **Rule 11(e)(1)(A) or (C)** agreement, and the guidelines *require* the court to delay acceptance of the plea agreement until the presentence report has been considered in most cases. **USSG §6B1.1(c).** Under the Guidelines, the court's acceptance of the plea is contingent on court's consideration of presentence report. *U.S. v. Cordova-Perez*, 65 F.3d 1552 (9th Cir.1995); *U.S. v. Kemper*, 908 F.2d 33, 36 (6th Cir.1990); *U.S. v. Foy*, 28 F.3d 464, 471 (5th Cir.1994); *U.S. v. Salva*, 902 F.2d 483, 488 (7th Cir..1990). Acceptance usually takes place on the record at the sentencing hearing, rather than at the change of plea hearing. Prior to *U.S. v. Hyde*, 520 U.S. 620, 117 S.Ct. 1630 (1997) some courts began to accept the plea agreement at the time of the plea hearing to prevent the defendant from withdrawing from the plea before sentencing. Defendants did so based on *U.S. v. Washman*, 66 F.3d 210 (9th Cir. 1996), which held that either party should be entitled to modify its position and even withdraw from the bargain until the plea is tendered and the bargain as it then exists is accepted by the court. Washman in turn relied on *U.S. v. Ocanas*, 628 F.2d 353, 358 (5th Cir.1980), cert. denied, 451 U.S. 984, 101 S.Ct. 2316, 68 L.Ed.2d 840 (1981) which held that unless and until the trial judge approves a plea agreement and accepts a guilty plea, neither party is bound by the agreement. The controversy was laid to rest when the Supreme Court held that once a plea is entered a defendant may not withdraw his plea unless he shows a fair and just reason under **Rule 32(e)** . *Hyde, supra* at 117 S.Ct.1631.

The sequence of events is important. **Rule 32** prohibits the court from reviewing the presentence report (PSR) before the guilty plea is accepted, and thus the court may not consider it in deciding whether to accept the plea (absent consent of the defendant). *In re Ellis*, 356 f.3d 1198, 1212 (9th Cir. 2004) (Kozinski, J. concurring). Thus the court must accept the plea, then read the PSR, then reject the plea agreement if not satisfied. At that point it is up to the defendant to decide whether to withdraw the plea: the court may not vacate the plea on its own motion. *Id.* at 1200.

6 Collateral Consequences of Plea

There are numerous collateral consequences to pleading guilty. The right to vote, the right to bear arms, access to government benefits, and a host of other rights can be effected. Below I mention only three consequences that have been troublesome.

6.1 Loss of Right to Carry Firearms

A plea to a felony under federal law will preclude the defendant from bearing firearms under *18 U.S.C. §922(g) and §921(a)(20)*. There is no provision for restoration of this right for federal felons except for petitions to the Secretary of the Treasury under *18 U.S.C. §925(c)*, which are no longer being processed. A state cannot restore a federal felon s right to bear arms. *Beecham v. U.S.*, 511 U.S. 368 (1994).

6.2 Immigration Consequences

In *Padilla v. Kentucky*, 559 U.S. 356, 130 S.Ct. 1473, 176 L.Ed.2d 284 (2010), the Supreme Court held that the Sixth Amendment requires an attorney for a criminal defendant to provide advice about the risk of deportation arising from a guilty plea. The immigration consequences of a plea agreements are very complex and require particular care. Defense counsel must be aware that loss of status, deportation, and other immigration consequences may be even more severe than the criminal sanctions. Whenever the defendant has any kind of immigration status, the consequences of a plea on that status should be evaluated and explained to the defendant prior to the decision to plead. In some cases, pleas can be structured so as to minimize the ill effect on the client. (*But see, Janvier v. United States,* 793 F.2d 449, 455 (C.A.2 1986) *" Section 1251(b) of 8 U.S.C., however, provides that § 1251(a)(4) is inapplicable if the sentencing judge, either at the time of sentencing or within 30 days thereafter, and after giving due notice to the appropriate authorities, recommends against deportation)".*

6.3 Use of Plea Statements in Other Proceedings

Uncoerced statements made by a defendant in a tribal guilty plea may be used for impeachment purposes at his federal trial. *U.S. v. Tsinnijinnie*, 91 F.3d 1285 (9th Cir. 1996). The court reasoned that if statements taken in violation of Miranda, evidence seized in violation of the Fourth Amendment, and suppression hearing testimony of the defendant may all be used for impeachment at trial, then there is no

reason to treat statements made during a tribal plea any differently.

Section 7

Appendix 1

7.1 ASHCROFT MEMORANDUM SEPTEMBER 22, 2003
SUBJECT: Department Policy Concerning Charging Criminal Offenses, Disposition of Charges, and Sentencing
INTRODUCTION

The passage of the Sentencing Reform Act of 1984 was a watershed event in the pursuit of fairness and consistency in the federal criminal justice system. With the Sentencing Reform Act s creation of the United States Sentencing Commission and the subsequent promulgation of the Sentencing Guidelines, Congress sought to provide certainty and fairness in meeting the purposes of sentencing. *28 U.S.C. 0 991(b)(l)(B).* In contrast to the prior sentencing system - which was characterized by largely unfettered discretion, and by seemingly severe sentences that were often sharply reduced by parole - the Sentencing Reform Act and the Sentencing Guidelines sought to accomplish several important objectives: (1) to ensure honesty and transparency in federal sentencing; (2) to guide sentencing discretion, so as to narrow the disparity between sentences for similar offenses committed by similar offenders; and **(3)** to
provide for the imposition of appropriately different punishments for offenses of differing severity.

With the passage of the ***PROTECT Act*** earlier this year, Congress has reaffirmed its commitment to the principles of consistency and effective

86

deterrence that are embodied in the Sentencing Guidelines. The important sentencing reforms made by this legislation will help to ensure greater fairness and to eliminate unwarranted disparities. These vital goals, however, cannot be fully achieved without consistency on the part of federal prosecutors in the Department of Justice. Accordingly, it is essential to set forth clear policies designed to ensure

that all federal prosecutors adhere to the principles and objectives of the Sentencing Reform Act, the PROTECT Act, and the Sentencing Guidelines in their charging, case disposition, and sentencing practices.

The Department has previously issued various memoranda addressing Department policies with respect to charging, case disposition, and sentencing. Shortly after the constitutionality of the Sentencing Reform Act was sustained by the Supreme Court in 1989, Attorney General Thornburgh issued a directive to federal prosecutors to ensure that their practices were consistent with the principles of equity, fairness, and uniformity. Several years later, Attorney General Reno issued additional guidance to address the extent to which a prosecutor s individualized assessment of the proportionality of particular sentences could be considered.

The recent passage of the **PROTECT Act** emphatically reaffirms Congress intention that the Sentencing Reform Act and the Sentencing Guidelines be faithfully and consistently enforced. It is therefore appropriate at this time to re-examine the subject thoroughly and to state with greater clarity Department policy with respect to charging, disposition of charges, and sentencing. One part of this comprehensive review of Department policy has already been completed: on July 28, 2003, in accordance with section 401(1)(1) of the **PROTECT Act,** I issued a

Memorandum that specifically and clearly sets forth the Department s policies with respect to sentencing recommendations and sentencing appeals. The determination of an appropriate sentence for a convicted defendant is, however, only half of the equation. The fairness Congress sought to achieve by the Sentencing Reform Act and the **PROTECT Act** can be attained only if there are fair and reasonably consistent policies with respect to the Department s decisions concerning what charges to bring and how cases should be disposed. Just as the sentence a defendant receives should not depend upon which particular judge presides over the case, so too the charges a defendant faces should not depend upon the particular prosecutor assigned to handle the case. Accordingly, the purpose of this Memorandum is to set forth basic policies that all federal prosecutors must follow in order to ensure that the Department fulfills its legal obligation to enforce faithfully and honestly the Sentencing Reform Act, the **PROTECT Act**, and the Sentencing Guidelines. This memorandum supersedes all previous guidance on this subject.

I. Department Policy Concerning Charging and Prosecution of Criminal Offenses

A. General Duty to Charge and to Pursue the Most Serious, Readily Provable Offense in All Federal Prosecutions

It is the policy of the Department of Justice that, in all federal criminal cases, federal prosecutors must charge and pursue the most serious, readily provable offense or offenses that are supported by the facts of the case, except as authorized by an Assistant Attorney General, United States

Attorney, or designated supervisory attorney in the limited circumstances described below. The most serious offense or offenses are those that generate the most substantial sentence under the Sentencing Guidelines, unless a mandatory minimum sentence or count requiring a consecutive sentence would generate a longer sentence. A charge is not readily provable if the prosecutor has a good faith doubt, for legal or evidentiary reasons, as to the Government s ability readily to prove a charge at trial. Thus, charges should not be filed simply to exert leverage to induce a plea. Once filed, the most serious readily provable charges may not be dismissed except to the extent permitted in Section B.

B. Limited Exceptions

The basic policy set forth above requires federal prosecutors to charge and to pursue all charges
that are determined to be readily provable and that, under the applicable statutes and Sentencing Guidelines, would yield the most substantial sentence. There are, however, certain limited exceptions to this requirement:

1. *Sentence would not be affected.* First, if the applicable guideline range from which a sentence may be imposed would be unaffected, prosecutors may decline to charge or to pursue readily provable charges. However, if the most serious readily provable charge involves a mandatory minimum sentence that exceeds the applicable guideline range, counts essential to establish a mandatory minimum sentence must be charged and may not be dismissed, except to the extent provided elsewhere below.

2. Fast-track programs. With the passage of the *PROTECT Act,* Congress recognized the importance of early disposition or fast-track programs. Section 401(m)(2)(B) of the Act instructs the Sentencing Commission to promulgate, by October 27, 2003, a policy statement authorizing a downward departure of not more than 4 levels pursuant to an early disposition program *authorized by the Attorney General* and the United States Attorney. **Pub. L. No. 108-21, 8 401(m)(2)(B), 117 Stat. 650, 675 (2003)** (emphasis added). Although the *PROTECT Act* requirement of Attorney General authorization only applies by its terms to fast- track programs that rely on downward departures, the same requirement will also apply, as a matter of Department policy, to any fast-track program that relies on charge bargaining - *i.e.,* an expedited disposition program whereby the Government agrees to charge less than the most serious, readily provable offense. Such programs are intended to be exceptional and will be authorized only when clearly by local conditions within a district. The specific requirements for establishing and implementing a fast-track program are set forth at length in the Department s Principles for Implementing An Expedited or Fast-Track Prosecution Program. In those districts where an approved fast-track program has been established, charging decisions and disposition of charges must comply with those Principles and with the other requirements of the approved fast-track program.

3. *Post-indictment reassessment.* In cases where post-indictment circumstances cause a prosecutor to determine in good faith that the most serious offense is not readily provable, because of a change in the evidence or some other justifiable reason *(e.g.,* the unavailability of a witness or the need to protect the identity of a witness until he testifies against a more significant defendant), the prosecutor may dismiss the charge(s) with the written or otherwise documented approval of an Assistant Attorney General, United States Attorney, or designated supervisory attorney.

4. *Substantial assistance.* The preferred means to recognize a defendant s substantial assistance in the investigation or prosecution of another person is to charge the most serious readily provable offense and then to file an appropriate motion or motions under **U.S.S.G. 8 5K1.1, 18 U.S.C. 8 3553(e),** or Federal Rule of Criminal Rule of Procedure 35(b). -3- However, in rare circumstances, where necessary to obtain substantial assistance in an important investigation or prosecution, and with the written or otherwise documented approval of an Assistant Attorney General, United States Attorney, or designated supervisory attorney, a federal prosecutor may decline to charge or to pursue a readily provable charge as part of plea agreement that properly reflects the substantial assistance provided by the defendant in the investigation or prosecution of another person.

5. *Statutory enhancements.* The use of statutory enhancements is strongly encouraged, and federal prosecutors must therefore take affirmative steps to ensure that the increased penalties resulting from specific statutory enhancements, such as the filing of an information pursuant to *21 U.S.C. 3 851* or the filing of a charge under *18 U.S.C. §924(c),* are sought in all appropriate cases. **As** soon as reasonably practicable, prosecutors should ascertain whether the defendant is eligible for any such statutory enhancement. In many cases, however, the filing of such enhancements will mean that the statutory sentence exceeds the applicable Sentencing Guidelines range, thereby ensuring that the defendant will not receive any credit for acceptance of responsibility and will have no incentive to plead guilty. Requiring the pursuit of such enhancements to trial in every case could therefore have a significant effect on the allocation of prosecutorial resources within a given district. Accordingly, an Assistant Attorney General, United States Attorney, or designated supervisory attorney may authorize a prosecutor to forego the filing of a statutory enhancement, but *only* in the context of a negotiated plea agreement, and subject to the following additional requirements:

a. Such authorization must be written or otherwise documented and may be granted only after careful consideration of the factors set forth in Section 9-27.420 of the United States Attorneys Manual. In the context of a statutory enhancement that is based on prior criminal convictions, such as an enhancement under *21 U.S.C. 8 851*, such authorization may be granted only after giving particular consideration to the nature, dates, and circumstances of the prior convictions, and the extent to which they are probative of criminal propensity.

b. A prosecutor may forego or dismiss a charge of a violation of *18 U.S.C. §924(c)* only with the written or otherwise documented approval of an Assistant Attorney General, United States Attorney, or designated supervisory attorney, and subject to the following limitations:

(i) In all but exceptional cases or where the total sentence would not be affected, the first readily provable violation of *18 U.S.C. § 924(c)* shall be charged and pursued.

(ii) In cases involving three or more readily provable violations of *18U.S.C. § 924(c)* in which the predicate offenses are crimes of violence, federal prosecutors shall, in all but exceptional cases, charge and pursue the first two such violations.

6. *Other Exceptional Circumstances.* Prosecutors may decline to pursue or may dismiss readily provable charges in other exceptional circumstances with the written or otherwise documented approval of an Assistant Attorney General, United States Attorney, or designated supervisory attorney. This exception recognizes that the aims of the Sentencing Reform Act must be sought without ignoring the practical limitations of the federal criminal justice system. For example, a case-specific approval to dismiss charges in a particular case might be given because the United States Attorney s Office is particularly over-burdened, the duration of the trial would be exceptionally long, and proceeding to trial would significantly reduce the total number of cases disposed of by the office. However, such case-by-case exceptions should be rare; otherwise the goals of fairness and equity will be jeopardized.

II. Department Policy Concerning Plea Agreements

A. Written Plea Agreements

In felony cases, plea agreements should be in writing. If the plea agreement is not in writing, the agreement should be formally stated on the record. Written plea agreements will facilitate efforts by the Department of Justice and the Sentencing Commission to monitor compliance by federal prosecutors with Department policies and the Sentencing Guidelines. The ***PROTECT Act*** specifically requires the court, after sentencing, to provide a copy of the plea agreement to the Sentencing Commission. ***28 U.S.C.§***

994(w). Written plea agreements also avoid misunderstandings with regard to the terms that the parties have accepted.

B. Honesty in Sentencing

As set forth in my July 28,2003 Memorandum on Department Policies and Procedures Concerning Sentencing Recommendations and Sentencing Appeals, Department of Justice policy requires honesty in sentencing, both with respect to the facts and the law:

Any sentencing recommendation made by the United States in a particular case must honestly reflect the totality and seriousness of the defendant s conduct and must be fully consistent with the Guidelines and applicable statutes and with the readily provable facts about the defendant s history and conduct.

This policy applies fully to sentencing recommendations that are contained in plea agreements. The July **28** Memorandum further explains that this basic policy has several important implications. In particular, if readily provable facts are relevant to calculations under the Sentencing Guidelines, the prosecutor must disclose them to the court, including the Probation Office. Likewise, federal prosecutors may not fact bargain, or be party to any plea agreement that results in the sentencing court having less than a full understanding of all readily provable facts relevant to sentencing.

The current provision of the United States Attorneys Manual that addresses charging policy and that describes the circumstances in which a less serious charge may be appropriate includes the admonition that [a] negotiated plea which uses any of the options described in this section must be made known to the sentencing court. See **U.S.A.M. 0 9-**

27.300(B); see *also* **U.S.A.M. 8 9-27.400(B)** (it would be improper for a prosecutor to agree that a departure is in order, but to conceal the agreement in a charge bargain that is presented to a court as a fait accompli so that there is neither a record of nor judicial review of the departure). Although this Memorandum by its terms supersedes prior Department guidance on this subject, it remains Department policy that the sentencing court should be informed if a plea agreement involves a charge bargain. Accordingly, a negotiated plea that uses any of the options described in Section I(B)(2), (4), *(5),* or (6) must be made known to the court at the time of the plea hearing and at the time of sentencing, *i.e.,* the court must be informed that a more serious, readily provable offense was not charged or that an applicable statutory enhancement was not filed.

C. Charge Bargaining

Charges may be declined or dismissed pursuant to a plea agreement only to the extent consistent with the principles set forth in Section I of this Memorandum.

D. Sentence Bargaining

There are only two types of permissible sentence bargains.

1. *Sentences within the Sentencing Guidelines range.* Federal prosecutors may enter into a plea agreement for a sentence that is within the specified guideline range. For example, when the Sentencing Guidelines range is 18-24 months, a prosecutor may agree to recommend a sentence of 18 or 20 months rather than to argue for a sentence at the top of the range. Similarly, a prosecutor may agree to recommend a downward adjustment for acceptance of responsibility under **U.S.S.G. 9 3El.** 1 if the prosecutor concludes in good faith that the defendant is entitled to the adjustment.

2. *Departures.* In passing the ***PROTECT Act***, Congress has made clear its view that there have been too many downward departures from the Sentencing Guidelines, and it has instructed the Commission to take measures to ensure that the incidence of downward departures [is] substantially reduced. **Pub. L. No. 108-21, 0 401(m)(2)(A), 117 Stat. 650, 675 (2003).** The Department has a duty to ensure that the circumstances in which it will request or accede to downward departures in the future are properly circumscribed. Accordingly, federal prosecutors must not request or accede to a downward departure except in the limited circumstances specified in this memorandum and with authorization from an Assistant Attorney General, United States Attorney, or designated supervisory attorney. Likewise, except in such circumstances and with such authorization, prosecutors may not simply stand silent when a downward departure motion is made by the defendant. An Assistant Attorney General, United States Attorney, or designated supervisory attorney may authorize a prosecutor to request or accede to a downward departure at sentencing only in the following circumstances:

a. *Substantial assistance. Section 5K1*.1 of the Sentencing Guidelines provides that, upon motion by the Government, a court may depart from the guideline range. A substantial assistance motion must be based on assistance that is *substantial* to the Government s case. It is not appropriate to utilize substantial assistance motions as a case management tool to secure plea agreements and avoid trials.

b. *Fast-track programs.* Federal prosecutors may support a downward departure to the extent consistent with the Sentencing Guidelines and the Attorney General s Principles for Implementing An Expedited or Fast-Track Prosecution Program. The *PROTECT Act* specifically recognizes the importance of such programs by requiring the Sentencing Commission to promulgate a policy statement specifically authorizing such departures.

c. *Other downward departures.* As set forth in my July 28 Memorandum, [other than these two situations, however, Government acquiescence in a downward departure should be, as the Sentencing Guidelines Manual itself suggests, a rare occurrence[e]. *See* **U.S.S.G., Ch. 1, Pt. A, 1 (4)(b)**. Prosecutors must affirmatively oppose downward departures that are not supported by the facts and the law, and must not agree to stand silent with respect to such departures. In particular, downward departures that would violate the specific restrictions of the *PROTECT Act* should be vigorously opposed. Moreover, as stated above, Department of Justice policy requires honesty in sentencing. In those cases where federal prosecutors agree to support departures, they are expected to identify departures for the courts. For example, it would be improper for a prosecutor to agree that a departure is warranted, without disclosing such agreement, so that there is neither a record of nor judicial review of the departure.

In sum, plea bargaining must honestly reflect the totality and seriousness of the defendant s conduct, and any departure must be accomplished through the application of appropriate Sentencing Guideline provisions.

CONCLUSION

Federal criminal law and procedure apply equally throughout the United States. As the sole federal prosecuting entity, the Department of Justice has a unique obligation to ensure that all federal criminal cases are prosecuted according to the same standards. Fundamental fairness requires that all defendants prosecuted in the federal criminal justice system be subject to the same standards and treated in a consistent manner.

[remainder of page intentionally left blank]

7.2 ASHCROFT MEMORANDUM
September 22, 2003

SUBJECT: Department Principles for Implementing an Expedited Disposition or Fast-Track Prosecution Program in a District

Section 401(m)(2)(B) of the 2003 *Prosecutorial Remedies and Other Tools to end the Exploitation of Children Today Act (PROTECT Act)* instructs the Sentencing Commission to promulgate, by October 27, 2003, a policy statement authorizing a downward departure of not more than 4 levels pursuant to an early disposition program *authorized by the Attorney General* and the United States Attorney. Pub. L. No. 108-21, § 401(m)(2)(B), 117 Stat. 650,675 (2003). Although the PROTECT Act requirement of Attorney General authorization only applies by its terms to fast-track programs that rely on downward departures, the Memorandum I have issued on Department Policy Concerning Charging Criminal Offenses, Disposition of Charges, and Sentencing likewise requires Attorney General approval for any fast-track program that relies upon charge bargaining - *i.e.,* a program whereby the Government agrees to charge less than the most serious, readily provable offense. This memorandum sets forth the general criteria that must be satisfied in order to obtain Attorney General authorization for fast-track programs and the procedures by which U.S. Attorneys may seek such authorization.3

I. REQUIRED CRITERIA FOR ATTORNEY GENERAL AUTHORIZATION OF A FAST-TRACK PROGRAM.

Early disposition or fast-track programs are based on the premise that a defendant who promptly agrees to participate in such a program has saved the government significant and scarce resources that can be used in prosecuting other defendants and has demonstrated an acceptance of responsibility above and beyond what is already taken into account by the adjustments contained in **U.S.S.G.** circumstances, such as where the resources of a district would otherwise be significantly strained by the large volume of a particular category of cases. Such programs are not to be used simply to avoid the ordinary application of the Guidelines to a particular class of cases. **3E1.1**. These programs are properly reserved for Exceptional In order to obtain Attorney General authorization to implement a fast track program, the United States Attorney must submit a proposal that demonstrates that the requirement that a fast-track program be approved by the Attorney General under the *PROTECT Act* or under these Principles may also be satisfied by obtaining the approval of the Deputy Attorney General. *See 28 U.S.C. 5 510; 28 C.F.R. 5 0.15(a).*

(A) (1) the district confronts an exceptionally large number of a specific class of offenses within the district, and failure to handle such cases on an expedited or fast-track basis would significantly strain prosecutorial and judicial resources available in the district; or

(2) the district confronts some other exceptional local circumstance with respect to a specific class of cases that justifies expedited disposition of such cases;

(B) declination of such cases in favor of state prosecution is either unavailable or clearly unwarranted;

(C) the specific class of cases consists of ones that are highly repetitive and present substantially similar fact scenarios; and

(D) the cases do not involve an offense that has been designated by the Attorney General as a crime of violence. *See* ***28 C.F.R. 0 28.2*** (listing offenses designated by the Attorney General as crimes of violence for purposes of the DNA collection provisions of the ***USA PATRIOT Act***).

These criteria will ensure that fast-track programs are implemented only when warranted. Thus, these criteria specify more clearly the circumstances under which a fast-track program could properly be implemented based on the high incidence of a particular type of offense within a district - one of the dost commonly cited reasons for justifying fast-track programs. Paragraph (A)(2), however, does not foreclose the possibility that there may be some other exceptional local circumstance, other than the high incidence of a particular type of offense, that could conceivably warrant fast-track treatment.

II. REQUIREMENTS GOVERNING UNITED STATES ATTORNEY IMPLEMENTATION OF FAST-TRACK PROGRAMS.

Once a United States Attorney has obtained authorization from the Attorney General to implement a fast-track program with respect to a particular specified class of offenses, the United States Attorney may implement such program in the manner he or she deems appropriate for that district, provided that the program is otherwise consistent with the law, the Sentencing Guidelines, and Department regulations and policy. Any such program must include the following elements:

A. *Expedited disposition.* Within a reasonably prompt period after the filing of federal charges, to be determined based on the practice in the district, the Defendant must agree to plead guilty to an offense covered by the fast-track program.

B. *Minimum requirements for fast-track plea agreement.* The Defendant must enter into a written plea agreement that includes at least the following terms: i. The defendant agrees to a factual basis that accurately reflects his or her offense conduct; ii. The defendant agrees not to file any of the motions described in ***Rule 12(b)(3), Fed. R. Crim. P.*** The defendant agrees to waive appeal; and iv. The defendant agrees to waive the opportunity to challenge his or her conviction under 28 U.S.C. § 2255, except on the issue of ineffective assistance of counsel.

C. *Additional provisions of plea agreement.* In exchange for the above, the attorney for the Government may agree to move at sentencing for a downward departure from the adjusted base offense level found by the District Court (after application of the adjustment for acceptance of responsibility) of a specific number of levels, not to exceed 4 levels. The plea agreement may commit the departure to the discretion of the district court, or the parties may agree to bind the district court to a specific number of levels, up to four levels, pursuant to ***Rule 1 l(c)(l)(C), Fed. R. Crim. P***. A charge bargaining fast- track program should provide for sentencing reductions that are commensurate with the foregoing. The parties may otherwise agree to the application of the Sentencing Guidelines consistently with the provisions of the Sentencing Guidelines and **Rule 11.**

III. PROCEDURES WITH RESPECT TO IMPLEMENTATION OF FAST-TRACK PROGRAMS.

Procedures for Attorney General approval. Before implementing a fast-track program, a district must submit to the Director of the Executive Office for United States Attorneys (EOUSA), for Attorney General approval, its proposal to implement a fast-track program. Likewise, any such program in existence on the date of this Memorandum may not be continued after October 27, 2003, unless a fast-track proposal has been submitted and approved. Any fast- track proposal must contain the following elements:

A. An identification of the specific category of violations to be covered by the fast-track program.

B. A detailed explanation of why the criteria described in Section I are satisfied with respect to such offenses. If the district has previously implemented a fast-track program for such offenses *(i.e.,* prior to the date of this memorandum).

Appendix "A"

U.S. Attorneys Manual
9-27.000

PRINCIPLES OF FEDERAL PROSECUTION

9-27.001

Preface

These principles of Federal prosecution provide to Federal prosecutors a statement of sound prosecutorial policies and practices for particularly important areas of their work. As such, it should promote the reasoned exercise of prosecutorial authority and contribute to the fair, evenhanded administration of the Federal criminal laws.

The manner in which Federal prosecutors exercise their decision-making authority has far-reaching implications, both in terms of justice and effectiveness in law enforcement and in terms of the consequences for individual citizens. A determination to prosecute represents a policy judgment that the fundamental interests of society require the application of the criminal laws to a particular set of circumstances—recognizing both that serious violations of Federal law must be prosecuted, and that prosecution entails profound consequences for the accused and the family of the accused whether or not a conviction ultimately results. Other prosecutorial decisions can be equally significant. Decisions, for example, regarding the specific charges to be brought, or concerning plea dispositions, effectively determine the range of sanctions that may be imposed for criminal conduct. The rare decision to consent to pleas of nolo contendere may affect the success of related civil suits for recovery of damages. Also, the government's position during the sentencing process will help assure that the court imposes a sentence consistent with the Sentencing Reform Act.

These principles of Federal prosecution have been designed to assist in structuring the decision-making process of attorneys for the government. For the most part, they have been cast in general terms with a view to providing guidance rather than to mandating results. The intent is to assure regularity without regimentation, to prevent unwarranted disparity without sacrificing necessary flexibility.

The availability of this statement of principles to Federal law enforcement officials and to the public serves two important purposes: ensuring the fair and effective exercise of prosecutorial responsibility by attorneys for the government, and promoting confidence on the part of the public and individual defendants that important prosecutorial decisions will be made rationally and objectively on the merits of each case. The Principles provide convenient reference points for the process of making prosecutorial decisions; they facilitate the task of training new attorneys in the proper discharge of their duties; they contribute to more effective management of the government's limited prosecutorial resources by promoting greater consistency among the prosecutorial activities of all United States Attorney's offices and between their activities and the Department's law enforcement priorities; they make possible better coordination of investigative and prosecutorial activity by enhan cing the understanding of investigating departments and agencies of the considerations underlying prosecutorial decisions by the Department; and they inform the public of the careful process by which prosecutorial decisions are made.

Important though these principles are to the proper operation of our Federal prosecutorial system, the success of that system must rely ultimately on the character, integrity, sensitivity, and competence of those men and women who are selected to represent the public interest in the Federal criminal justice process. It is with their help that these principles have been prepared, and it is with their efforts that the purposes of these principles will be achieved.

These principles were originally promulgated by Attorney General Benjamin R. Civiletti on July 28, 1980. While they have since been updated to reflect changes in the law and current policy of the Department of Justice, the underlying message to Federal prosecutors remains unchanged.

9-27.110

Purpose

The principles of Federal prosecution set forth herein are intended to promote the reasoned exercise of prosecutorial discretion by attorneys for the government with respect to:

Initiating and declining prosecution;

Selecting charges;

Entering into plea agreements;

Opposing offers to plead nolo contendere;

Entering into non-prosecution agreements in return for cooperation; and

Participating in sentencing.

Comment. Under the Federal criminal justice system, the prosecutor has wide latitude in determining when, whom, how, and even whether to prosecute for apparent violations of Federal criminal law. The prosecutor's broad discretion in such areas as initiating or foregoing prosecutions, selecting or recommending specific charges, and terminating prosecutions by accepting guilty pleas has been recognized on numerous occasions by the courts. See, e.g., Oyler v. Boles, 368 U.S. 448 (1962); Newman v. United States, 382 F.2d 479 (D.C. Cir. 1967); Powell v. Ratzenbach, 359 F.2d 234 (D.C. Cir. 1965), cert. denied, 384 U.S. 906 (1966). This discretion exists by virtue of his/her status as a member of the Executive Branch, which is charged under the Constitution with ensuring that the laws of the United States be "faithfully executed." U.S. Const. Art. § 3. See Nader v. Saxbe, 497 F.2d 676, 679 n. 18 (D.C. Cir. 1974).

Since Federal prosecutors have great latitude in making crucial decisions concerning enforcement of a nationwide system of criminal justice, it is desirable, in the interest of the fair and effective administration of justice in the Federal system, that all Federal prosecutors be guided by a general statement of principles that summarizes appropriate considerations to be weighed, and desirable practices to be followed, in discharging their prosecutorial responsibilities.

Although these principles deal with the specific situations indicated, they should be read in the broader context of the basic responsibilities of Federal attorneys: making certain that the general purposes of the criminal law—assurance of warranted punishment, deterrence of further criminal conduct, protection of the public from dangerous offenders, and rehabilitation of offenders—are adequately met, while making certain also that the rights of individuals are scrupulously protected.

[cited in USAM 9-2.031]

9-27.120

Application

In carrying out criminal law enforcement responsibilities, each Department of Justice attorney should be guided by the principles set forth herein, and each United States Attorney and each Assistant Attorney General should ensure that such principles are communicated to the attorneys who exercise prosecutorial responsibility within his/her office or under his/her direction or supervision.

Comment. It is expected that each Federal prosecutor will be guided by these principles in carrying out his/her criminal law enforcement responsibilities unless a modification of, or departure from, these principles has been authorized pursuant to USAM 9-27.140. See also Criminal Resource Manual 792 ("Incentives for Subjects and Targets of Criminal Investigations and Defendants in Criminal Cases to Provide Foreign Intelligence Information"). However, it is not intended that reference to these principles will require a particular prosecutorial decision in any given case. Rather, these principles are set forth solely for the purpose of assisting attorneys for the government in determining how best to exercise their authority in the performance of their duties.

[updated January 2007]

9-27.130

Implementation

Each United States Attorney (USA) and responsible Assistant Attorney General should establish internal office procedures to ensure:

That prosecutorial decisions are made at an appropriate level of responsibility, and are made consistent with these principles; and

That serious, unjustified departures from the principles set forth herein are followed by such remedial action, including the imposition of disciplinary sanctions, when warranted, as are deemed appropriate.

Comment. Each USA and each Assistant Attorney General responsible for the enforcement of Federal criminal law should supplement the guidance provided by the principles set forth herein by establishing appropriate internal procedures for his/her office. One purpose of such procedures should be to ensure consistency in the decisions within each office by regularizing the decision making process so that decisions are made at the appropriate level of responsibility. A second purpose, equally important, is to provide appropriate remedies for serious, unjustified departures from sound prosecutorial principles. The USA or Assistant Attorney General may also wish to establish internal procedures for appropriate review and documentation of decisions.

9-27.140

Modifications or Departures

United States Attorneys (USA) may modify or depart from the principles set forth herein as necessary in the interests of fair and effective law enforcement within the district. Any significant modification or departure contemplated as a matter of policy or regular practice must be approved by the appropriate Assistant Attorney General and the Deputy Attorney General.

Comment. Although these materials are designed to promote consistency in the application of Federal criminal laws, they are not intended to produce rigid uniformity among Federal prosecutors in all areas of the country at the expense of the fair administration of justice. Different offices face different conditions and have different requirements. In recognition of these realities, and in order to maintain the flexibility necessary to respond fairly and effectively to local conditions, each USA is specifically authorized to modify or depart from the principles set forth herein, as necessary in the interests of fair and effective law enforcement within the district. In situations in which a modification or departure is contemplated as a matter of policy or regular practice, the appropriate Assistant Attorney General and the Deputy Attorney General must approve the action before it is adopted.

[cited in USAM 9-27.120]
9-27.150

Non-Litigability

The principles set forth herein, and internal office procedures adopted pursuant hereto, are intended solely for the guidance of attorneys for the government. They are not intended to, do not, and may not be relied upon to create a right or benefit, substantive or procedural, enforceable at law by a party to litigation with the United States.

Comment. This statement of principles has been developed purely as matter of internal Departmental policy and is being provided to Federal prosecutors solely for their own guidance in performing their duties. Neither this statement of principles nor any internal procedures adopted by individual offices pursuant hereto creates any rights or benefits. By setting forth this fact explicitly, USAM 9-27.150 is intended to foreclose efforts to litigate the validity of prosecutorial actions alleged to be at variance with these principles or not in compliance with internal office procedures that may be adopted pursuant hereto. In the event that an attempt is made to litigate any aspect of these principles, or to litigate any internal office procedures adopted pursuant to these materials, or to litigate the applicability of such principles or procedures to a particular case, the United States Attorney concerned should oppose the attempt and should notify the Department immediately.

9-27.200
Initiating and Declining Prosecution—Probable Cause Requirement

If the attorney for the government has probable cause to believe that a person has committed a Federal offense within his/her jurisdiction, he/she should consider whether to:

Request or conduct further investigation;

Commence or recommend prosecution;

Decline prosecution and refer the matter for prosecutorial consideration in another jurisdiction;

Decline prosecution and initiate or recommend pretrial diversion or other non-criminal disposition; or

Decline prosecution without taking other action.

Comment. USAM 9-27.220 sets forth the courses of action available to the attorney for the government once he/she has probable cause to believe that a person has committed a Federal offense within his/her jurisdiction. The probable cause standard is the same standard as that required for the issuance of an arrest warrant or a summons upon a complaint (See Fed. R. Crim. P. 4(a)), for a magistrate's decision to hold a defendant to answer in the district court (See Fed. R. Crim. P. 5.1(a)), and is the minimal requirement for indictment by a grand jury. See Branzburg v. Hayes, 408 U.S. 665, 686 (1972). This is, of course, a threshold consideration only. Merely because this requirement can be met in a given case does not automatically warrant prosecution; further investigation may be warranted, and the prosecutor should still take into account all relevant considerations, including those described in the following provis ions, in deciding upon his/her course of action. On the other hand, failure to meet the minimal requirement of probable cause is an absolute bar to initiating a Federal prosecution, and in some circumstances may preclude reference to other prosecuting authorities or recourse to non-criminal sanctions as well.

[cited in USAM 9-10.060; USAM 9-2.031]

9-27.220

Grounds for Commencing or Declining Prosecution

The attorney for the government should commence or recommend Federal prosecution if he/she believes that the person's conduct constitutes a Federal offense and that the admissible evidence will probably be sufficient to obtain and sustain a conviction, unless, in his/her judgment, prosecution should be declined because:

No substantial Federal interest would be served by prosecution;

The person is subject to effective prosecution in another jurisdiction; or

There exists an adequate non-criminal alternative to prosecution.

Comment. USAM 9-27.220 expresses the principle that, ordinarily, the attorney for the government should initiate or recommend Federal prosecution if he/she believes that the person's conduct constitutes a Federal offense and that the admissible evidence probably will be sufficient to obtain and sustain a conviction. Evidence sufficient to sustain a conviction is required under Rule 29(a), Fed. R. Crim. P., to avoid a judgment of acquittal. Moreover, both as a matter of fundamental fairness and in the interest of the efficient administration of justice, no prosecution should be initiated against any person unless the government believes that the person probably will be found guilty by an unbiased trier of fact. In this connection, it should be noted that, when deciding whether to prosecute, the government attorney need not have in hand all the evidence upon which he/she intends to rely at trial: it is sufficient that he/she have a reasonable be lief that such evidence will be available and admissible at the time of trial. Thus, for example, it would be proper to commence a prosecution though a key witness is out of the country, so long as the witness's presence at trial could be expected with reasonable certainty.

The potential that—despite the law and the facts that create a sound, prosecutable case—the factfinder is likely to acquit the defendant because of the unpopularity of some factor involved in the prosecution or because of the overwhelming popularity of the defendant or his/her cause, is not a factor prohibiting prosecution. For example, in a civil rights case or a case involving an extremely popular political figure, it might be clear that the evidence of guilt—viewed objectively by an unbiased factfinder—would be sufficient to obtain and sustain a conviction, yet the prosecutor might reasonably doubt whether the jury would convict. In such a case, despite his/her negative assessment of the likelihood of a guilty verdict (based on factors extraneous to an objective view of the law and the facts), the prosecutor may properly conclude that it is necessary and desirable to commence or recommend prosecution and allow the criminal process to operate in accordance with its principles.

Merely because the attorney for the government believes that a person's conduct constitutes a Federal offense and that the admissible evidence will be sufficient to obtain and sustain a conviction, does not mean that he/she necessarily should initiate or recommend prosecution: USAM 9-27.220 notes three situations in which the prosecutor may property decline to take action nonetheless: when no substantial Federal interest would be served by prosecution; when the person is subject to effective prosecution in another jurisdiction; and when there exists an adequate non-criminal alternative to prosecution. It is left to the judgment of the attorney for the government whether such a situation exists. In exercising that judgment, the attorney for the government should consult USAM 9-27.230, 9-27.240, or 9-27.250, as appropriate.

[cited in USAM 6-4.210; USAM 9-10.060; USAM 9-27.200; USAM 9-28.300]

9-27.230
Initiating and Declining Charges—Substantial Federal Interest

In determining whether prosecution should be declined because no substantial Federal interest would be served by prosecution, the attorney for the government should weigh all relevant considerations, including:

Federal law enforcement priorities;

The nature and seriousness of the offense;

The deterrent effect of prosecution;

The person's culpability in connection with the offense;

The person's history with respect to criminal activity;

The person's willingness to cooperate in the investigation or prosecution of others; and

The probable sentence or other consequences if the person is convicted.

Comment. USAM 9-27.230 lists factors that may be relevant in determining whether prosecution should be declined because no substantial Federal interest would be served by prosecution in a case in which the person is believed to have committed a Federal offense and the admissible evidence is expected to be sufficient to obtain and sustain a conviction. The

116

list of relevant considerations is not intended to be all-inclusive. Obviously, not all of the factors will be applicable to every case, and in any particular case one factor may deserve more weight than it might in another case.

Federal Law Enforcement Priorities. Federal law enforcement resources and Federal judicial resources are not sufficient to permit prosecution of every alleged offense over which Federal jurisdiction exists. Accordingly, in the interest of allocating its limited resources so as to achieve an effective nationwide law enforcement program, from time to time the Department establishes national investigative and prosecutorial priorities. These priorities are designed to focus Federal law enforcement efforts on those matters within the Federal jurisdiction that are most deserving of Federal attention and are most likely to be handled effectively at the Federal level. In addition, individual United States Attorneys may establish their own priorities, within the national priorities, in order to concentrate their resources on problems of particular local or regional significance. In weighing the Federal interest in a particular prosecution, the attorney for the government s hould give careful consideration to the extent to which prosecution would accord with established priorities.

Nature and Seriousness of Offense. It is important that limited Federal resources not be wasted in prosecuting inconsequential cases or cases in which the violation is only technical. Thus, in determining whether a substantial Federal interest exists that requires prosecution, the attorney for the government should consider the nature and seriousness of the offense involved. A number of factors may be relevant. One factor that is obviously of primary importance is the actual or potential impact of the offense on the community and on the victim.

The impact of an offense on the community in which it is committed can be measured in several ways: in terms of economic harm done to community interests; in terms of physical danger to the citizens or damage to public property; and in terms of erosion of the inhabitants' peace of mind and sense of security. In assessing the seriousness of the offense in these terms, the prosecutor may properly weigh such questions as whether the violation is technical or relatively inconsequential in nature and what the public attitude is toward prosecution under the circumstances of the case. The public may be indifferent, or even opposed, to enforcement of the controlling statute whether on substantive grounds, or because of a history of nonenforcement, or because the offense involves essentially a minor matter of private concern and the victim is not interested in having it pursued. On the other hand, the nature and circumstances of the offense, the identity of the offender or the victim, or t he attendant publicity, may be such as to create strong public sentiment in favor of prosecution. While public interest, or lack thereof, deserves the prosecutor's careful attention, it should not be used to justify a decision to prosecute, or to take other action, that cannot be supported on other grounds. Public and professional responsibility sometimes will require the choosing of a particularly unpopular course.

Economic, physical, and psychological considerations are also important in assessing the impact of the offense on the victim. In this connection, it is appropriate for the prosecutor to take into account such matters as the victim's age or health, and whether full or partial restitution has been made. Care should be taken in weighing the matter of restitution, however, to ensure against contributing to an impression that an offender can escape prosecution merely by returning the spoils of his/her crime.

Deterrent Effect of Prosecution. Deterrence of criminal conduct, whether it be criminal activity generally or a specific type of criminal conduct, is one of the primary goals of the criminal law. This purpose should be kept in mind, particularly when deciding whether a prosecution is warranted for an offense that appears to be relatively minor; some offenses, although seemingly not of great importance by themselves, if commonly committed would have a substantial cumulative impact on the community.

The Person's Culpability. Although the prosecutor has sufficient evidence of guilt, it is nevertheless appropriate for him/her to give consideration to the degree of the person's culpability in connection with

118

the offenses, both in the abstract and in comparison with any others involved in the offense. If for example, the person was a relatively minor participant in a criminal enterprise conducted by others, or his/her motive was worthy, and no other circumstances require prosecution, the prosecutor might reasonably conclude that some course other than prosecution would be appropriate.

The Person's Criminal History. If a person is known to have a prior conviction or is reasonably believed to have engaged in criminal activity at an earlier time, this should, be considered in determining whether to initiate or recommend Federal prosecution. In this connection particular attention should be given to the nature of the person's prior criminal involvement, when it occurred, its relationship if any to the present offense, and whether he/she previously avoided prosecution as a result of an agreement not to prosecute in return for cooperation or as a result of an order compelling his/her testimony. By the same token, a person's lack of prior criminal involvement or his/her previous cooperation with the law enforcement officials should be given due consideration in appropriate cases.

The Person's Willingness to Cooperate. A person's willingness to cooperate in the investigation or prosecution of others is another appropriate consideration in the determination whether a Federal prosecution should be undertaken. Generally speaking, a willingness to cooperate should not by itself relieve a person of criminal liability. There may be some cases, however, in which the value of a person's cooperation clearly outweighs the Federal interest in prosecuting him/her. These matters are discussed more fully below, in connection with plea agreements and non-prosecution agreements in return for cooperation.

The Person's Personal Circumstances. In some cases, the personal circumstances of an accused may be relevant in determining whether to prosecute or to take other action. Some circumstances peculiar to the accused, such as extreme youth, advanced age, or mental or physical impairment, may suggest that prosecution is not the most appropriate

119

response to his/her offense; other circumstances, such as the fact that the accused occupied a position of trust or responsibility which he/she violated in committing the offense, might weigh in favor of prosecution.

The Probable Sentence. In assessing the strength of the Federal interest in prosecution, the attorney for the government should consider the sentence, or other consequence, that is likely to be imposed if prosecution is successful, and whether such a sentence or other consequence would justify the time and effort of prosecution. If the offender is already subject to a substantial sentence, or is already incarcerated, as a result of a conviction for another offense, the prosecutor should weigh the likelihood that another conviction will result in a meaningful addition to his/her sentence, might otherwise have a deterrent effect, or is necessary to ensure that the offender's record accurately reflects the extent of his/her criminal conduct. For example, it might be desirable to commence a bail-jumping prosecution against a person who already has been convicted of another offense so that law enforcement personnel and judicial officers who encounter him/her in the future wil l be aware of the risk of releasing him/her on bail. On the other hand, if the person is on probation or parole as a result of an earlier conviction, the prosecutor should consider whether the public interest might better be served by instituting a proceeding for violation of probation or revocation of parole, than by commencing a new prosecution. The prosecutor should also be alert to the desirability of instituting prosecution to prevent the running of the statute of limitations and to preserve the availability of a basis for an adequate sentence if there appears to be a chance that an offender's prior conviction may be reversed on appeal or collateral attack. Finally, if a person previously has been prosecuted in another jurisdiction for the same offense or a closely related offense, the attorney for the government should consult existing departmental policy statements on the subject of "successive prosecution" or "dual prosecution," depending on whether the earlier prosecution w as Federal or nonfederal. See USAM 9-2.031 (Petite Policy).

Just as there are factors that are appropriate to consider in determining whether a substantial Federal interest would be served by prosecution in a particular case, there are considerations that deserve no weight and should not influence the decision. These include the time and resources expended in Federal investigation of the case. No amount of investigative effort warrants commencing a Federal prosecution that is not fully justified on other grounds.

[cited in USAM 9-2.031; USAM 9-27.220]

9-27.240
Initiating and Declining Charges—Prosecution in Another Jurisdiction

In determining whether prosecution should be declined because the person is subject to effective prosecution in another jurisdiction, the attorney for the government should weigh all relevant considerations, including:

The strength of the other jurisdiction's interest in prosecution;
The other jurisdictions ability and willingness to prosecute effectively; and

The probable sentence or other consequences if the person is convicted in the other jurisdiction.

Comment. In many instances, it may be possible to prosecute criminal conduct in more than one jurisdiction. Although there may be instances in which a Federal prosecutor may wish to consider deferring to prosecution in another Federal district, in most instances the choice will probably be between Federal prosecution and prosecution by state or local authorities. USAM 9-27.240 sets forth three general considerations to be taken into account in determining whether a person is likely to be prosecuted effectively in another jurisdiction: the strength of the jurisdiction's interest in prosecution; its ability and willingness to prosecute effectively; and the probable sentence or other consequences if the person is convicted. As indicated with respect to the considerations listed in paragraph 3, these factors are illustrative only, and the attorney for the government should also consider any others that appear relevant to his/her in a particular cas e.

The Strength of the Jurisdiction's Interest. The attorney for the government should consider the relative Federal and state characteristics of the criminal conduct involved. Some offenses, even though in violation of Federal law, are of particularly strong interest to the authorities of the state or local jurisdiction in which they occur, either because of the nature of the offense, the identity of the offender or victim, the fact that the investigation was conducted primarily by state or local investigators, or some other circumstance. Whatever the reason, when it appears that the Federal interest in prosecution is less substantial than the interest of state or local authorities, consideration should be given to referring the case to those authorities rather than commencing or recommending a Federal prosecution.

Ability and Willingness to Prosecute Effectively. In assessing the likelihood of effective prosecution in another jurisdiction, the attorney for the government should also consider the intent of the authorities in that jurisdiction and whether that jurisdiction has the prosecutorial and judicial resources necessary to undertake prosecution promptly and effectively. Other relevant factors might be legal or evidentiary problems that might attend prosecution in the other jurisdiction. In addition, the Federal prosecutor should be alert to any local conditions, attitudes, relationships, or other circumstances that might cast doubt on the likelihood of the state or local authorities conducting a thorough and successful prosecution.

Probable Sentence Upon Conviction. The ultimate measure of the potential for effective prosecution in another jurisdiction is the sentence, or other consequence, that is likely to be imposed if the person is convicted. In considering this factor, the attorney for the government should bear in mind not only the statutory penalties in the jurisdiction and sentencing patterns in similar cases, but also, the particular characteristics of the offense or, of the offender that might be relevant to sentencing. He/she should also be alert to the possibility that a conviction under state law may, in some cases result in collateral consequences for the defendant, such as disbarment, that might not follow upon a conviction under Federal law.

[cited in USAM 5-11.113; USAM 9-27.220; USAM 9-28.1100]

9-27.250
Non-Criminal Alternatives to Prosecution

In determining whether prosecution should be declined because there exists an adequate, non-criminal alternative to prosecution, the attorney for the government should consider all relevant factors, including:

The sanctions available under the alternative means of disposition;

The likelihood that an effective sanction will be imposed; and

The effect of non-criminal disposition on Federal law enforcement interests.

Comment. When a person has committed a Federal offense, it is important that the law respond promptly, fairly, and effectively. This does not mean, however, that a criminal prosecution must be initiated. In recognition of the fact that resort to the criminal process is not necessarily the only appropriate response to serious forms of antisocial activity, Congress and state legislatures have provided civil and administrative remedies for many types of conduct that may also be subject to criminal sanction. Examples of such non-criminal approaches include civil tax proceedings; civil actions under the securities, customs, antitrust, or other regulatory laws; and reference of complaints to licensing authorities or to professional organizations such as bar associations. Another potentially useful alternative to prosecution in some cases is pretrial diversion. See USAM 9-22.000.

Attorneys for the government should familiarize themselves with these alternatives and should consider pursuing them if they are available in a particular case. Although on some occasions they should be pursued in addition to the criminal law procedures, on other occasions they can be expected to provide an effective substitute for criminal prosecution. In weighing the adequacy of such an alternative in a particular case, the prosecutor should consider the nature and severity of the sanctions that could be imposed, the likelihood that an adequate sanction would in fact be imposed, and the effect of such a non-criminal disposition on Federal law enforcement interests. It should be noted that referrals for non-criminal disposition may not include the transfer of grand jury material unless an order under Rule 6(e), Federal Rules of Criminal Procedure, has been obtained. See United States v. Sells Engineering, Inc., 463 U.S. 418 (1983).

[cited in USAM 9-27.220; USAM 9-28.1100]

9-27.260
Initiating and Declining Charges—Impermissible Considerations

In determining whether to commence or recommend prosecution or take other action against a person, the attorney for the government should not be influenced by:

The person's race, religion, sex, national origin, or political association, activities or beliefs;

The attorney's own personal feelings concerning the person, the person's associates, or the victim; or

The possible affect of the decision on the attorney's own professional or personal circumstances.

Comment. USAM 9-27.260 sets forth various matters that plainly should not influence the determination whether to initiate or recommend prosecution or take other action. They are listed here not because it is anticipated that any attorney for the government might allow them to affect his/her judgment, but in order to make clear that Federal prosecutors will not be influenced by such improper considerations. Of course, in a case in which a particular characteristic listed in subparagraph (1) is pertinent to the offense (for example, in an immigration case the fact that the offender is not a United States national, or in a civil rights case the fact that the victim and the offender are of different races), the provision would not prohibit the prosecutor from considering it for the purpose intended by the Congress.

[cited in USAM 8-3.300]

9-27.270

Records of Prosecutions Declined

Whenever the attorney for the government declines to commence or recommend Federal prosecution, he/she should ensure that his/her decision and the reasons therefore are communicated to the investigating agency involved and to any other interested agency, and are reflected in the office files.

Comment. USAM 9-27.270 is intended primarily to ensure an adequate record of disposition of matters that are brought to the attention of the government attorney for possible criminal prosecution, but that do not result in Federal prosecution. When prosecution is declined in serious cases on the understanding that action will be taken by other authorities, appropriate steps should be taken to ensure that the matter receives their attention and to ensure coordination or follow-up.

9-27.300

Selecting Charges—Charging Most Serious Offenses

Except as provided in USAM 9-27.330, (pre-charge plea agreements), once the decision to prosecute has been made, the attorney for the government should charge, or should recommend that the grand jury charge, the most serious offense that is consistent with the nature of the defendant's conduct, and that is likely to result in a sustainable conviction. If mandatory minimum sentences are also involved, their effect must be considered, keeping in mind the fact that a mandatory minimum is statutory and generally overrules a guideline. The "most serious" offense is generally that which yields the highest range under the sentencing guidelines.

However, a faithful and honest application of the Sentencing Guidelines is not incompatible with selecting charges or entering into plea agreements on the basis of an individualized assessment of the extent to which particular charges fit the specific circumstances of the case, are consistent with the purposes of the Federal criminal code, and maximize the impact of Federal resources on crime. Thus, for example, in determining "the most serious offense that is consistent with the nature of the defendant's conduct that is likely to result in a sustainable conviction," it is appropriate that the attorney for the government consider, inter alia, such factors as the Sentencing Guideline range yielded by the charge, whether the penalty yielded by such sentencing range (or potential mandatory minimum charge, if applicable) is proportional to the seriousness of the defendant's conduct, and whether the charge achieves such purposes of the criminal law as punishment, protection of the pub lic, specific and general deterrence, and rehabilitation. Note that these factors may also be considered by the attorney for the government when entering into plea agreements. USAM 9-27.400.

To ensure consistency and accountability, charging and plea agreement decisions must be made at an appropriate level of responsibility and documented with an appropriate record of the factors applied.

Comment. Once it has been determined to initiate prosecution, either by filing a complaint or an information, or by seeking an indictment from the grand jury, the attorney for the government must determine what charges to file or recommend. When the conduct in question consists of a single criminal act, or when there is only one applicable statute, this is not a difficult task. Typically, however, a defendant will have committed more than one criminal act and his/her conduct may be prosecuted under more than one statute. Moreover, selection of charges may be complicated further by the fact that different statutes have different proof requirements and provide substantially different penalties. In such cases, considerable care is required to ensure selection of the proper charge or charges. In addition to reviewing the concerns that prompted the decision to prosecute in the first instance, particular attention should be given to the need to ensure that the prosecution will be b oth fair and effective.

At the outset, the attorney for the government should bear in mind that at trial he/she will have to produce admissible evidence sufficient to obtain and sustain a conviction or else the government will suffer a dismissal. For this reason, he/she should not include in an information or recommend in an indictment charges that he/she cannot reasonably expect to prove beyond a reasonable doubt by legally sufficient evidence at trial.

In connection with the evidentiary basis for the charges selected, the prosecutor should also be particularly mindful of the different requirements of proof under different statutes covering similar conduct. For example, the bribe provisions of 18 U.S.C. § 201 require proof of "corrupt intent," while the "'gratuity" provisions do not. Similarly, the "two witness" rule applies to perjury prosecutions under 18 U.S.C. § 1621 but not under 18 U.S.C. § 1623.

As stated, a Federal prosecutor should initially charge the most serious, readily provable offense or offenses consistent with the defendant's conduct. Charges should not be filed simply to exert leverage to induce a plea, nor should charges be abandoned in an effort to arrive at a bargain that fails to reflect the seriousness of the defendant's conduct.

USAM 9-27.300 expresses the principle that the defendant should be charged with the most serious offense that is encompassed by his/her conduct and that is readily provable. Ordinarily, as noted above this will be the offense for which the most severe penalty is provided by law and the guidelines. Where two crimes have the same statutory maximum and the same guideline range, but only one contains a mandatory minimum penalty, the one with the mandatory minimum is the more serious. This principle provides the framework for ensuring equal justice in the prosecution of Federal criminal offenders. It guarantees that every defendant will start from the same position, charged with the most serious criminal act he/she commits. Of course, he/she may also be charged with other criminal acts (as provided in USAM 9-27.320), if the proof and the government's legitimate law enforcement objectives warrant additional charges . Current drug laws provide for increased maximum, and in some cases minimum, penalties for many offenses on the basis of a defendant's prior criminal convictions. See, e.g., 21 U.S.C. §§ 841 (b)(1)(A),(B), and (C), 848(a), 960 (b)(1), (2), and (3), and 962. However, a court may not impose such an increased penalty unless the United States Attorney has filed an information with the court, before trial or before entry of a plea of guilty, setting forth the previous convictions to be relied upon 21 U.S.C. § 851.

Every prosecutor should regard the filing of an information under 21 U.S.C. § 851 concerning prior convictions as equivalent to the filing of charges. Just as a prosecutor must file a readily provable charge, he or she must file an information under 21 U.S.C. § 851 regarding prior convictions that are readily provable and that are known to the prosecutor prior to the beginning of trial or entry of plea. The only exceptions to this requirement are where: (1) the failure to file or the dismissal of such pleadings would not affect the applicable guideline range from which the sentence may be imposed; or (2) in the context of a negotiated plea, the United States Attorney, the Chief Assistant United States Attorney, the senior supervisory Criminal Assistant United States Attorney or within the Department of Justice, a Section Chief or Office Director has approved the negotiated agreement. The reasons for such an agreement must be set forth in writing. Such a reason might i nclude, for example, that the United

128

States Attorney's office is particularly overburdened, the case would be time-consuming to try, and proceeding to trial would significantly reduce the total number of cases disposed of by the office. The permissible agreements within this context include: (1) not filing an enhancement; (2) filing an enhancement which does not allege all relevant prior convictions, thereby only partially enhancing a defendant's potential sentence; and (3) dismissing a previously filed enhancement.

A negotiated plea which uses any of the options described in this section must be made known to the sentencing court. In addition, the sentence which can be imposed through the negotiated plea must adequately reflect the seriousness of the offense.

Prosecutors are reminded that when a defendant commits an armed bank robbery or other crime of violence or drug trafficking crime, appropriate charges include 18 U.S.C. § 924 (c).

[cited in USAM 9-27.400; USAM 9-28.1200; USAM 9-100.020]

9-27.320
Additional Charges

Except as hereafter provided, the attorney for the government should also charge, or recommend that the grand jury charge, other offenses only when, in his/her judgment, additional charges:

Are necessary to ensure that the information or indictment:
Adequately reflects the nature and extent of the criminal conduct involved; and

Provides the basis for an appropriate sentence under all the circumstances of the case; or

Will significantly enhance the strength of the government's case against the defendant or a codefendant.

Comment. It is important to the fair and efficient administration of justice in the Federal system that the government bring as few charges as are necessary to ensure that justice is done. The bringing of unnecessary charges not only complicates and prolongs trials, it constitutes an excessive—and potentially unfair—exercise of power. To ensure appropriately limited exercises of the charging power, USAM 9-27.320 outlines three general situations in which additional charges may be brought: (1) when necessary adequately to reflect the nature and extent of the criminal conduct involved; (2) when necessary to provide the basis for an appropriate sentence under all the circumstances of the case; and (3) when an additional charge or charges would significantly strengthen the case against the defendant or a codefendant.

Nature and Extent of Criminal Conduct. Apart from evidentiary considerations, the prosecutor's initial concern should be to select charges that adequately reflect the nature and extent of the criminal conduct involved. This means that the charges selected should fairly describe both the kind and scope of unlawful activity; should be legally sufficient; should provide notice to the public of the seriousness of the conduct involved; and should negate any impression that, after committing one offense, an offender can commit others with impunity.

Basis for Sentencing. Proper charge selection also requires consideration of the end result of successful prosecution—the imposition of an appropriate sentence under all the circumstances of the case. In order to achieve this result, it ordinarily should not be necessary to charge a person with every offense for which he/she, may technically be liable (indeed, charging every such offense may in some cases be perceived as an unfair attempt to induce a guilty plea). What is important is that the person be charged in such a manner that, if he/she is convicted, the court may impose an appropriate sentence. Under the sentencing guidelines, if the offense actually charged bears a true relationship with the defendant's conduct, an appropriate guideline sentence will follow. However, the prosecutor must take care to be sure that the charges brought allow the guidelines to operate properly. For instance, charging a significant participant in a major drug conspiracy only with u sing a communication facility would result in a sentence which, even if it were the maximum possible under the charged offense, would be artificially low given the defendant's actual conduct.

Effect on the Government's Case. When considering whether to include a particular charge in the indictment or information, the attorney for the government should bear in mind the possible effects of inclusion or exclusion of the charge on the government's case against the defendant or a codefendant. If the evidence is available, it is proper to consider the tactical advantages of bringing certain charges. For example, in a case in which a substantive offense was committed pursuant to an unlawful agreement, inclusion of a conspiracy count is permissible and may be desirable to ensure the introduction of all relevant evidence at trial. Similarly, it might be important to include a perjury or false statement count in an indictment charging other offenses, in order to give the jury a complete picture of the defendant's criminal conduct. Failure to include appropriate charges for which the proof is sufficient may not only result in the exclusion, of relevant evidence, but ma y impair the prosector's ability to prove a coherent case, and lead to jury confusion as well. In this connection, it is important to remember that, in multi-defendant cases, the presence or absence of a particular charge against one defendant may affect the strength of the case against another defendant. In short, when the evidence exists, the charges should be structured so as to permit proof of the strongest case possible without undue burden on the administration of justice.

[cited in USAM 6-4.210; USAM 9-27.300]

9-27.330

Pre-Charge Plea Agreements

Before filing or recommending charges pursuant to a precharge plea agreement, the attorney for the government should consult the plea agreement provisions of USAM 9-27.430, thereof, relating to the selection of charges to which a defendant should be required to plead guilty.

[cited in USAM 9-27.300]

9-27.400

Plea Agreements Generally

The attorney for the government may, in an appropriate case, enter into an agreement with a defendant that, upon the defendant's plea of guilty or nolo contendere to a charged offense or to a lesser or related offense, he/she will move for dismissal of other charges, take a certain position with respect to the sentence to be imposed, or take other action. Plea agreements, and the role of the courts in such agreements, are addressed in Chapter Six of the Sentencing Guidelines. See also USAM 9-27.300 which discusses the individualized assessment by prosecutors of the extent to which particular charges fit the specific circumstances of the case, are consistent with the purposes of the Federal criminal code, and maximize the impact of Federal resources on crime.

Comment. USAM 9-27.400 permits, in appropriate cases, the disposition of Federal criminal charges pursuant to plea agreements between defendants and government attorneys. Such negotiated dispositions should be distinguished from situations in which a defendant pleads guilty or nolo contendere to fewer than all counts of an information or indictment in the absence of any agreement with the government. Only the former type of disposition is covered by the provisions of USAM 9-27.400 et seq.

Negotiated plea dispositions are explicitly sanctioned by Rule 11(e)(1), Fed. R. Crim. P., which provides that:

The attorney for the government and the attorney for the defendant or the defendant when acting pro se may engage in discussions with a view toward reaching an agreement that upon the entering of a plea of guilty or nolo contendere to a charged offense or to a lesser or related offense, the attorney for the government will do any of the following:

Move for dismissal of other charges; or

Make a recommendation, or agree not to oppose, the defendant's request for a particular sentence, with the understanding that such recommendation or request shall not be binding upon the court; or

Agree that a specific sentence is the appropriate disposition of the case.

Three types of plea agreements are encompassed by the language of USAM 9-27.400, agreements whereby in return for the defendant's plea to a charged offense or to a lesser or related offense, other charges are dismissed ("charge agreements"); agreements pursuant to which the government takes a certain position regarding the sentence to be imposed ("sentence agreements"); and agreements that combine a plea with a dismissal of charges and an undertaking by the prosecutor concerning the government's position at sentencing ("mixed agreements").

Once prosecutors have indicted, they should not find themselves bargaining about charges which they have determined are readily provable and reflect the seriousness of the defendant's conduct. Charge agreements envision dismissal of counts in exchange for a plea. As with the indictment decision, the prosecutor should seek a plea to the most serious readily provable offense charged. Should a prosecutor determine in good faith after indictment that, as a result of a change in the evidence or for another reason (e.g., a need has arisen to protect the identity of a particular witness until he or she testifies against a more significant defendant), a charge is not readily provable or that an indictment exaggerates the seriousness of an offense or offenses, a plea bargain may reflect the prosecutor's reassessment. There should be documentation, however, in a case in which charges originally brought are dropped.

The language of USAM 9-27.400 with respect to sentence agreements is intended to cover the entire range of positions that the government might wish to take at the time of sentencing. Among the options are: taking no position regarding the sentence; not opposing the defendant's request; requesting a specific type of sentence (e.g., a fine or probation), a specific fine or term of imprisonment, or not more than a specific fine or term of imprisonment; and requesting concurrent rather than consecutive sentences. Agreement to any such option must be consistent with the guidelines.

There are only two types of sentence bargains. Both are permissible, but one is more complicated than the other. First, prosecutors may bargain for a sentence that is within the specified United States Sentencing Commission's guideline range. This means that when a guideline range is 18 to 24 months, the prosecutor has discretion to agree to recommend a sentence of 18 to 20 months rather than to argue for a sentence at the top of the range. Such a plea does not require that the actual sentence range be determined in advance. The plea agreement may have wording to the effect that once the range is determined by the court, the United States will recommend a low point in that range. Similarly, the prosecutor may agree to recommend a downward adjustment for acceptance of responsibility if he or she concludes in good faith that the defendant is entitled to the adjustment. Second, the prosecutor may seek to depart from the guidelines. This is more complicated than a bargain involving a sentence within a guideline range. Departures are discussed more generally below.

Department policy requires honesty in sentencing; Federal prosecutors are expected to identify for the court departures when they agree to support them. For example, it would be improper for a prosecutor to agree that a departure is in order, but to conceal the agreement in a charge bargain that is presented to a court as a fait accompli so that there is neither a record of nor judicial review of the departure.

Plea bargaining, both charge bargaining and sentence bargaining, must honestly reflect the totality and seriousness of the defendant's conduct and any departure to which the prosecutor is agreeing, and must be accomplished through appropriate guideline provisions.

The basic policy is that charges are not to be bargained away or dropped, unless the prosecutor has a good faith doubt as to the government's ability readily to prove a charge for legal or evidentiary reasons. There are, however, two exceptions.

First, if the applicable guideline range from which a sentence may be imposed would be unaffected, readily provable charges may be dismissed or dropped as part of a plea bargain. It is important to know whether dropping a charge may affect a sentence. For example, the multiple offense rules in Part D of Chapter 3 of the guidelines and the relevant conduct standard set forth in Sentencing Guideline 1B1.3(a)(2) will mean that certain dropped charges will be counted for purposes of determining the sentence, subject to the statutory maximum for the offense or offenses of conviction. It is vital that Federal prosecutors understand when conduct that is not charged in an indictment or conduct that is alleged in counts that are to be dismissed pursuant to a bargain may be counted for sentencing purposes and when it may not be. For example, in the case of a defendant who could be charged with five bank robberies, a decision to charge only one or to dismiss four counts pursuant to a bar gain precludes any consideration of the four uncharged or dismissed robberies in determining a guideline range, unless the plea agreement included a stipulation as to the other robberies. In contrast, in the case of a defendant who could be charged with five counts of fraud, the total amount of money involved in a fraudulent scheme will be considered in determining a guideline range even if the defendant pleads guilty to a single count and there is no stipulation as to the other counts.

Second, Federal prosecutors may drop readily provable charges with the specific approval of the United States Attorney or designated supervisory level official for reasons set forth in the file of the case. This exception recognizes that the aims of the Sentencing Reform Act must be sought without ignoring other, critical aspects of the Federal criminal justice system. For example, approvals to drop charges in a particular case might be given because the United States Attorney's office is particularly over-burdened, the case would be time-consuming to try, and proceeding to trial would significantly reduce the total number of cases disposed of by the office.

In Chapter 5, Part K of the Sentencing Guidelines, the Commission has listed departures that may be considered by a court in imposing a sentence. Moreover, Guideline 5K2.0 recognizes that a sentencing court may consider a ground for departure that has not been adequately considered by the Commission. A departure requires approval by the court. It violates the spirit of the guidelines and Department policy for prosecutor to enter into a plea bargain which is based upon the prosecutor's and the defendant's agreement that a departure is warranted, but that does not reveal to the court the existence of the departure and thereby afford the court an opportunity to reject it.

The Commission has recognized those bases for departure that are commonly justified. Accordingly, before the government may seek a departure based on a factor other than one set forth in Chapter 5, Part X, approval of the United States Attorney or designated supervisory officials is required. This approval is required whether or not a case is resolved through a negotiated plea.

Section 5K1.1 of the Sentencing Guidelines allows the United States to file a pleading with the sentencing court which permits the court to depart below the indicated guideline, on the basis that the defendant provided substantial assistance in the investigation or prosecution of another. Authority to approve such pleadings is limited to the United States Attorney, the Chief Assistant United States Attorney, and supervisory criminal Assistant United States Attorneys, or a committee including at least one of these individuals. Similarly, for Department of Justice attorneys, approval authority should be vested in a Section Chief or Office

Director, or such official's deputy, or in a committee which includes at least one of these individuals.

Every United States Attorney or Department of Justice Section Chief or Office Director shall maintain documentation of the facts behind and justification for each substantial assistance pleading. The repository or repositories of this documentation need not be the case file itself. Freedom of Information Act considerations may suggest that a separate form showing the final decision be maintained.

The procedures described above shall also apply to Motions filed pursuant to Rule 35(b), Federal Rules of Criminal Procedure, where the sentence of a cooperating defendant is reduced after sentencing on motion of the United States. Such a filing is deemed for sentencing purposes to be the equivalent of a substantial assistance pleading.

The concession required by the government as part of a plea agreement, whether it be a "charge agreement," a "sentence agreement," or a "mixed agreement," should be weighed by the responsible government attorney in the light of the probable advantages and disadvantages of the plea disposition proposed in the particular case. Particular care should be exercised in considering whether to enter into a plea agreement pursuant to which the defendant will enter a nolo contendere plea. As discussed in USAM 9-27.500 and USAM 9-16.000, there are serious objections to such pleas and they should be opposed unless the responsible Assistant Attorney General concluded that the circumstances are so unusual that acceptance of such a plea would be in the public interest.

[updated September 2000] [cited in USAM 9-16.300; USAM 9-16.320; USAM 9-27.300; USAM 9-28.1300]

9-27.420

Plea Agreements—Considerations to be Weighed

In determining whether it would be appropriate to enter into a plea agreement, the attorney for the government should weigh all relevant considerations, including:

The defendant's willingness to cooperate in the investigation or prosecution of others;

The defendant's history with respect to criminal activity;

The nature and seriousness of the offense or offenses charged;

The defendant's remorse or contrition and his/her willingness to assume responsibility for his/her conduct;

The desirability of prompt and certain disposition of the case;

The likelihood of obtaining a conviction at trial;

The probable effect on witnesses;

The probable sentence or other consequences if the defendant is convicted;

The public interest in having the case tried rather than disposed of by a guilty plea;

The expense of trial and appeal;

The need to avoid delay in the disposition of other pending cases; and

The effect upon the victim's right to restitution.

Comment. USAM 9-27.420 sets forth some of the appropriate considerations to be weighed by the attorney for the government in deciding whether to enter into a plea agreement with a defendant pursuant to the provisions of Rule 11(e), Fed. R. Crim. P. The provision is not intended to suggest the desirability or lack of desirability of a plea agreement in any particular case or to be construed as a reflection on the merits of any plea agreement that actually may be reached; its purpose is solely to assist attorneys for the government in exercising their judgment as to whether some sort of plea agreement would be appropriate in a particular case. Government attorneys should consult the investigating agency involved and the victim, if appropriate or required by law, in any case in which it would be helpful to have their views concerning the relevance of particular factors or the weight they deserve.

Defendant's Cooperation. The defendant's willingness to provide timely and useful cooperation as part of his/her plea agreement should be given serious consideration. The weight it deserves will vary, of course, depending on the nature and value of the cooperation offered and whether the same benefit can be obtained without having to make the charge or sentence concession that would be involved in a plea agreement. In many situations, for example, all necessary cooperation in the form of testimony can be obtained through a compulsion order under 18 U.S.C.§§ 6001-6003. In such cases, that approach should be attempted unless, under the circumstances, it would seriously interfere with securing the person's conviction. If the defendant's cooperation is sufficiently substantial to justify the filing of a 5K1.1 Motion for a downward departure, the procedures set out in USAM 9-27.400(B) shall be followed.

Defendant's Criminal History. One of the principal arguments against the practice of plea bargaining is that it results in leniency that reduces the deterrent impact of the law and leads to recidivism on the part of some offenders. Although this concern is probably most relevant in non-federal jurisdictions that must dispose of large volumes of routine cases with inadequate resources, nevertheless it should be kept in mind by Federal prosecutors, especially when dealing with repeat offenders or "career

Daniel Storm

criminals." Particular care should be taken in the case of a defendant with a prior criminal record to ensure that society's need for protection is not sacrificed in the process of arriving at a plea disposition. In this connection, it is proper for the government attorney to consider not only the defendant's past, but also facts of other criminal involvement not resulting in conviction. By the same token, of course, it is also proper to consider a defendant's absence of past criminal involvement and his/her past cooperation with law enforcement officials. Note that 18 U.S.C.§ 924(e), as well as Sentencing Guidelines 4B1.1 and 4B1.4 address "career criminals" and "armed career criminals." 18 U.S.C. § 3559(c)—the so-called "three strikes" statute—addresses serious violent recidivist offenders. The application of these provisions to a particular case may affect the plea negotiation posture of the parties.

Nature and Seriousness of Offense Charged. Important considerations in determining whether to enter into a plea agreement may be the nature and seriousness of the offense or offenses charged. In weighing those factors, the attorney for the government should bear in mind the interests sought to be protected by the statute defining the offense (e.g., the national defense, constitutional rights, the governmental process, personal safety, public welfare, or property), as well as nature and degree of harm caused or threatened to those interests and any attendant circumstances that aggravate or mitigate the seriousness of the offense in the particular case.

Defendant's Attitude. A defendant may demonstrate apparently genuine remorse or contrition, and a willingness to take responsibility for his/her criminal conduct by, for example, efforts to compensate the victim for injury or loss, or otherwise to ameliorate the consequences of his/her acts. These are factors that bear upon the likelihood of his/her repetition of the conduct involved and that may properly be considered in deciding whether a plea agreement would be appropriate. Sentencing Guideline 3E1.1 allows for a downward adjustment upon acceptance of responsibility by the defendant. It is permissible for a prosecutor to enter a plea agreement which approves such an adjustment if the defendant otherwise meets the requirements of the section.

It is particularly important that the defendant not be permitted to enter a guilty plea under circumstances that will allow him/her later to proclaim lack of culpability or even complete innocence. Such consequences can be avoided only if the court and the public are adequately informed of the nature and scope of the illegal activity and of the defendant's complicity and culpability. To this end, the attorney for the government is strongly encouraged to enter into a plea agreement only with the defendant's assurance that he/she will admit, the facts of the offense and of his/her culpable participation therein. A plea agreement may be entered into in the absence of such an assurance, but only if the defendant is willing to accept without contest a statement by the government in open court of the facts it could prove to demonstrate his/her guilt beyond a reasonable doubt. Except as provided in USAM 9-27.440, the attorney for the government should not enter into a plea agreement with a defendant who admits his/her guilt but disputes an essential element of the government's case.

Prompt Disposition. In assessing the value of prompt disposition of a criminal case, the attorney for the government should consider the timing of a proffered plea. A plea offer by a defendant on the eve of trial after the case has been fully prepared is hardly as advantageous from the standpoint of reducing public expense as one offered months or weeks earlier. In addition, a last minute plea adds to the difficulty of scheduling cases efficiently and may even result in wasting the prosecutorial and Judicial time reserved for the aborted trial. For these reasons, governmental attorneys should make clear to defense counsel at an early stage in the proceedings that, if there are to be any plea discussions, they must be concluded prior to a certain date well in advance of the trial date. See USSG § 3E1.1(b)(1). However, avoidance of unnecessary trial preparation and scheduling disruptions are not the only benefits to be gained from prompt disposition of a case by means of a guilty plea. Such a disposition also saves the government and the court the time and expense of trial and appeal. In addition, a plea agreement facilitates prompt imposition of sentence, thereby promoting the overall goals of the criminal justice system. Thus, occasionally it may be appropriate to enter into a plea agreement even after the usual time for making such agreements has passed.

Likelihood of Conviction. The trial of a criminal case inevitably involves risks and uncertainties, both for the prosecution and for the defense. Many factors, not all of which can be anticipated, can affect the outcome. To the extent that these factors can be identified, they should be considered in deciding whether to accept a plea or go to trial. In this connection, the prosecutor should weigh the strength of the government's case relative to the anticipated defense case, bearing in mind legal and evidentiary problems that might be expected, as well as the importance of the credibility of witnesses. However, although it is proper to consider factors bearing upon the likelihood of conviction in deciding whether to enter into a plea agreement, it obviously is improper for the prosecutor to attempt to dispose of a case by means of a plea agreement if he/she is not satisfied that the legal standards for guilt are met.

Effect on Witnesses. Attorneys for the government should bear in mind that it is often burdensome for witnesses to appear at trial and that sometimes to do so may cause them serious embarrassment or even place them in jeopardy of physical or economic retaliation. The possibility of such adverse consequences to witnesses should not be overlooked in determining whether to go to trial or attempt to reach a plea agreement. Another possibility that may have to be considered is revealing the identity of informants. When an informant testifies at trial, his/her identity and relationship to the government become matters of public record. As a result, in addition to possible adverse consequences to the informant, there is a strong likelihood that the informant's usefulness in other investigations will be seriously diminished or destroyed. These are considerations that should be discussed with the investigating agency involved, as well as with any other agencies known to have an interest in using the informant in their investigations.

Probable Sentence. In determining whether to enter into a plea agreement, the attorney for the government may properly consider the probable outcome of the prosecution in terms of the sentence or other consequences for the defendant in the event that a plea agreement is reached. If the proposed agreement is a "sentence agreement" or a "mixed agreement," the prosecutor should realize that the position he/she agrees to take with respect to sentencing may have a significant effect on the sentence that is actually imposed. If the proposed agreement is a "charge agreement," the prosecutor should bear in mind the extent to which a plea to fewer or lesser offenses may reduce the sentence that otherwise could be imposed. In either event, it is important that the attorney for the government be aware of the need to preserve the basis for an appropriate sentence under all the circumstances of the case. Thorough knowledge of the Sentencing Guidelines, any applicable statutory minim um sentences, and any applicable sentence enhancements is clearly necessary to allow the prosecutor to accurately and adequately evaluate the effect of any plea agreement.

Trial Rather Than Plea. There may be situations in which the public interest might better be served by having a case tried rather than by having it disposed of by means of a guilty plea. These include situations in which it is particularly important to permit a clear public understanding that "justice is done" through exposing the exact nature of the defendant's wrongdoing at trial, or in which a plea agreement might be misconstrued to the detriment of public confidence in the criminal justice system. For this reason, the prosecutor should be careful not to place undue emphasis on factors which favor disposition of a case pursuant to a plea agreement.

Expense of Trial and Appeal. In assessing the expense of trial and appeal that would be saved by a plea disposition, the attorney for the government should consider not only such monetary costs as juror and witness fees, but also the time spent by judges, prosecutors, and law enforcement personnel who may be needed to testify or provide other assistance at trial. In this connection, the prosecutor should bear in mind the complexity of the case, the number of trial days and witnesses required, and any extraordinary expenses that might be incurred such as the cost of sequestering the jury.

Prompt Disposition of Other Cases. A plea disposition in one case may facilitate the prompt disposition of other cases, including cases in which prosecution might otherwise be declined. This may occur simply because prosecutorial, judicial, or defense resources will become available for use in other cases, or because a plea by one of several defendants may have a "domino effect," leading to pleas by other defendants. In weighing the importance of these possible consequences, the attorney for the government should consider the state of the criminal docket and the speedy trial requirements in the district, the desirability of handling a larger volume of criminal cases, and the work loads of prosecutors, judges, and defense attorneys in the district.

[cited in USAM 9-28.1300]

9-27.430

Selecting Plea Agreement Charges

If a prosecution is to be concluded pursuant to a plea agreement, the defendant should be required to plead to a charge or charges:

That is the most serious readily provable charge consistent with the nature and extent of his/her criminal conduct;

That has an adequate factual basis;

That makes likely the imposition of an appropriate sentence and order of restitution, if appropriate, under all the circumstances of the case; and

That does not adversely affect the investigation or prosecution of others.

Comment. USAM 9-27.430 sets forth the considerations that should be taken into account in selecting the charge or charges to which a defendant should be required to plead guilty once it has been decided to dispose of the case pursuant to a plea agreement. The considerations are essentially the same as those governing the selection of charges to be included in the original indictment or information. See USAM 9-27.300.

Relationship to Criminal Conduct. The charge or charges to which a defendant pleads guilty should be consistent with the defendant's criminal conduct, both in nature and in scope. Except in unusual circumstances, this charge will be the most serious one, as defined in USAM 9-27.300. This principle governs the number of counts to which a plea should be required in cases involving different offenses, or in cases involving a series of familiar offenses. Therefore the prosecutor must be familiar with the Sentencing Guideline rules applicable to grouping offenses (Guideline 3D) and to relevant conduct (USSG § 1B1.3) among others. In regard to the seriousness of the offense, the guilty plea should assure that the public record of conviction provides an adequate indication of the defendant's conduct. With respect to the number of counts, the prosecutor should take care to assure that no impression is given that multiple offenses are li kely to result in no greater a potential penalty than is a single offense. The requirement that a defendant plead to a charge, that is consistent with the nature and extent of his/her criminal conduct is not inflexible. Although cooperation is usually acknowledged through a Sentencing Guideline 5K1.1 filing, there may be situations involving cooperating defendants in which considerations such as those discussed in USAM 9-27.600, take precedence. Such situations should be approached cautiously, however. Unless the government has strong corroboration for the cooperating defendant's testimony, his/her credibility may be subject to successful impeachment if he/she is permitted to plead to an offense that appears unrelated in seriousness or scope to the charges against the defendants on trial. It is also doubly important in such situations for the prosecutor to ensure that the public record of the plea demonstrates, the full extent of the defendant's i nvolvement in the criminal activity, giving rise to the prosecution.

Factual Basis. The attorney for the government should also bear in mind the legal requirement that there be a factual basis for the charge or charges to which a guilty plea is entered. This requirement is intended to assure against conviction after a guilty plea of. a person who is not in fact guilty. Moreover, under Rule 11(f) of the Fed. R. Crim. P., a court may not enter a judgment upon a guilty plea "without making such inquiry as shall satisfy it that, there is a factual basis for the plea." For this reason, it is essential that the charge or charges selected as the subject of a plea agreement be such as could be prosecuted independently of the plea under these principles. However, as noted, in cases in which Alford or nolo contendere pleas are tendered, the attorney for the government may wish to make a stronger factual showing. In such cases there may remain some doubt as to the defendant's guilt even after the entry of his/her plea. Consequently, in order to a void such a misleading impression, the government should ask leave of the court to make a proffer of the facts available to it that show the defendant's guilt beyond a reasonable doubt.

In addition, the Department's policy is only to stipulate to facts that accurately represent the defendant's conduct. If a prosecutor wishes to support a departure from the guidelines, he or she should candidly do so and not stipulate to facts that are untrue. Stipulations to untrue facts are unethical. If a prosecutor has insufficient facts to contest a defendant's effort to seek a downward departure or to claim an adjustment, the prosecutor can say so. If the presentence report states facts that are inconsistent with a stipulation in which a prosecutor has joined, the prosecutor should object to the report or add a statement explaining the prosecutor's understanding of the facts or the reason for the stipulation.

Recounting the true nature of the defendant's involvement in a case will not always lead to a higher sentence. Where a defendant agrees to cooperate with the government by providing information concerning unlawful activities of others and the government agrees that self-incriminating information so provided will not be used against the defendant, Sentencing Guideline 1B1.8 provides that the information shall not be used in determining the applicable guideline range, except to the

146

extent provided in the agreement. The existence of an agreement not to use information should be clearly reflected in the case file, the applicability of Guideline 1B1.8 should be documented, and the incriminating information must be disclosed to the court or the probation officer, even though it may not be used in determining a guideline sentence. Note that such information may still be used by the court in determining whether to depart from the guidelines and the extent of the departure. See US SG § 1B1.8.

Basis for Sentencing. In order to guard against inappropriate restriction of the court's sentencing options, the plea agreement should provide adequate scope for sentencing under all the circumstances of the case. To the extent that the plea agreement requires the government to take a position with respect to the sentence to be imposed, there should be little danger since the court will not be bound by the government's position. When a "charge agreement" is involved, however, the court will be limited to imposing the maxim term authorized by statue as well as the Sentencing Guideline range for the offense, to which the guilty plea is entered. Thus, as noted in USAM 9-27.320 above the prosecutor should take care to avoid a "charge agreement" that would unduly restrict the court's sentencing authority. In this connection, as in the initial selection of charges, the prosecutor should take into account the purposes of sentencing, the penalti es provided in the applicable statutes (including mandatory minimum penalties), the gravity of the offense, any aggravating or mitigating factors, and any post conviction consequences to which the defendant may be subject. In addition, if restitution is appropriate under the circumstances of the case, the plea agreement should specify the amount of restitution. See 18 U.S.C. § 3663 et seq.; 18 U.S.C. §§ 2248, 2259, 2264 and 2327; United States v. Arnold, 947 F.2d 1236, 1237-38 (5th Cir. 1991); and USAM 9-16.320.

Effect on Other Cases. In a multiple-defendant case, care must be taken to ensure that the disposition of the charges against one defendant does not adversely affect the investigation or prosecution of co-defendants. Among the possible adverse consequences to be avoided are the negative jury appeal that may result when relatively less culpable defendants are tried in the absence of a more culpable defendant or when a principal prosecution witness appears to be equally culpable as the defendants but has been permitted to plead to a significantly less serious offense; the possibility that one defendant's absence from the case will render useful evidence inadmissible at the trial of co-defendants; and the giving of questionable exculpatory testimony on behalf of the other defendants by the defendant who has pled guilty.

9-27.440

Plea Agreements When Defendant Denies Guilt

The attorney for the government should not, except with the approval of the Assistant Attorney General with supervisory responsibility over the subject matter, enter into a plea agreement if the defendant maintains his/her innocence with respect to the charge or charges to which he/she offers to plead guilty. In a case in which the defendant tenders a plea of guilty but denies committing the offense to which he/she offers to plead guilty, the attorney for the government should make an offer of proof of all facts known to the government to support the conclusion that the defendant is in fact guilty. See also USAM 9-16.015, which discusses the approval requirement.

Comment. USAM 9-27.440 concerns plea agreements involving "Alford" pleas—guilty pleas entered by defendants who nevertheless claim to be innocent. In North Carolina v. Alford, 400 U.S. 25 (1970), the Supreme Court held that the Constitution does not prohibit a court from accepting a guilty plea from a defendant who simultaneously maintains his/her innocence, so long as the plea is entered voluntarily and intelligently and there is a strong factual basis for it. The Court reasoned that there is no material difference between a plea of nolo contendere, where the defendant does not expressly admit his/her guilt, and a plea of guilty by a defendant who affirmatively denies his/her guilt.

Despite the constitutional validity of Alford pleas, such pleas should be avoided except in the most unusual circumstances, even if no plea agreement is involved and the plea would cover all pending charges. Such pleas are particularly undesirable when entered as part of an agreement with the government. Involvement by attorneys for the government in the inducement of guilty pleas by defendants who protest their innocence may create an appearance of prosecutorial overreaching. As one court put it, "the public might well not understand or accept the fact that a defendant who denied his guilt was nonetheless placed in a position of pleading guilty and going to jail." See United States v. Bednarski, 445 F.2d 364, 366 (1st Cir. 1971). Consequently, it is preferable to have a jury resolve the factual and legal dispute between the government and the defendant, rather than have government attorneys encourage defendants to plead guilty under circumstances that the public might regard as questionable or unfair. For this reason, government attorneys should not enter into Alford plea agreements, without the approval of the responsible Assistant Attorney General. Apart from refusing to enter into a plea agreement, however, the degree to which the Department can express its opposition to Alford pleas may be limited. Although a court may accept a proffered plea of nolo contendere "only after due consideration of the views of the parties and the interest of the public in the effective administration of justice" (Rule 11 (b), Fed. R. Crim. P.), at least one court has concluded that it is an abuse of discretion to refuse to accept a guilty plea "solely because the defendant does not admit the alleged facts of the crime." United States v. Gaskins, 485 F.2d 1046, 1048 (D.C. Cir. 1973); see United States v. Bednarski, supra; United States v. Boscoe, 518 F.2d 95 (1st Cir. 1975). Nevertheless, government attorneys can and should discourage Alford pleas by refusing to agree to terminate prosecutions where an Alford plea is proffered to fewer than all of the charges pending. As is the case with guilty pleas generally, if such a plea to fewer than all the charges is tendered and accepted over the government's objection, the attorney for the government should proceed to trial on any remaining charges not barred on double jeopardy grounds unless the United States Attorney or in cases handled by Departmental attorneys, the responsible Assistant Attorney General, approves dismissal of those charges.

Government attorneys should also take full advantage of the opportunity afforded by Rule 11(f) of the Fed. R. Crim. P. in an Alford case to thwart the defendant's efforts to project a public image of innocence. Under Rule 11(f) of the Fed. R. Crim. P. the court must be satisfied that there is "a factual basis" for a guilty plea. However, the Rule does not require that the factual basis for the plea be provided only by the defendant. See United States v. Navedo, 516 F.2d 29 (2d Cir. 1975); Irizarry v. United States, 508 F.2d 960 (2d Cir. 1974); United States v. Davis, 516 F.2d 574 (7th Cir. 1975). Accordingly, attorneys for the government in Alford cases should endeavor to establish as strong a factual basis for the plea as possible not only to satisfy the requirement of Rule 11(f) Fed. R. Crim. P., but also to minimize the adverse effects of Alford pleas on public perceptions of the administration of justice.

[updated September 2006] [cited in USAM 6-4.330; USAM 9-28.1300]

9-27.450

Records of Plea Agreements

All negotiated plea agreements to felonies or to misdemeanors negotiated from felonies shall be in writing and filed with the court.

Comment. USAM 9-27.450 is intended to facilitate compliance with Rule 11 of the Federal Rules of Criminal Procedure and to provide a safeguard against misunderstandings that might arise concerning the terms of a plea agreement. Rule 11(e) (2), Fed. R. Crim. P., requires that a plea agreement be disclosed in open court (except upon a showing of good cause in which case disclosure may be made in camera), while Rule 11(e)(3) Fed. R. Crim. P. requires that the disposition provided for in the agreement be embodied in the judgment and sentence. Compliance with these requirements will be facilitated if the agreement has been reduced to writing in advance, and the defendant will be precluded from successfully contesting the terms of the agreement at the time he/she pleads guilty, or at the time of sentencing, or at a later date. Any time a defendant enters into a negotiated plea, that fact and the conditions of the agreement should also be maintained i n the office case file. Written agreements will facilitate efforts by the Department or the Sentencing Commission to monitor compliance by prosecutors with Department policies and the guidelines. Documentation may include a copy of the court transcript at the time the plea is taken in open court.

There shall be within each office a formal system for approval of negotiated pleas. The approval authority shall be vested in at least a supervisory criminal Assistant United States Attorney, or a supervisory attorney of a litigating division in the Department of Justice, who will have the responsibility of assessing the appropriateness of the plea agreement under the policies of the Department of Justice pertaining to pleas. Where certain predictable fact situations arise with great frequency and are given identical treatment, the approval requirement may be met by a written instruction from the appropriate supervisor which describes with particularity the standard plea procedure to be followed, so long as that procedure is otherwise within Departmental guidelines. An example would be a border district which routinely deals with a high volume of illegal alien cases daily.

The plea approval process will be part of the office evaluation procedure.

The United States Attorney in each district, or a supervisory representative, should, if feasible, meet regularly with a representative of the district's Probation Office for the purpose of discussing guideline cases.

9-27.500
Offers to Plead Nolo Contendere—Opposition Except in Unusual Circumstances

The attorney for the government should oppose the acceptance of a plea of nolo contendere unless the Assistant Attorney General with supervisory responsibility over the subject matter concludes that the circumstances of the case are so unusual that acceptance of such a plea would be in the public interest. See USAM 9-16.010, which discusses the approval requirement.

Comment. Rule 11(b) of the Federal Rules of Criminal Procedure, requires the court to consider "the views of the parties and the interest of the public in the effective administration of justice" before it accepts a plea of nolo contendere. Thus it is clear that a criminal defendant has no absolute right to enter a nolo contendere plea. The Department has long attempted to discourage the disposition of criminal cases by means of nolo pleas. The basic objections to nolo pleas were expressed by Attorney General Herbert Brownell, Jr. in a Departmental directive in 1953.

One of the factors which has tended to breed contempt for Federal law enforcement in recent times has been the practice of permitting as a matter of course in many criminal indictments the plea of nolo contendere. While it may serve a legitimate purpose in a few extraordinary situations and where civil litigation is also pending, I can see no justification for it as an everyday practice, particularly where it is used to avoid certain indirect consequences of pleading guilty, such as loss of license or sentencing as a multiple offender. Uncontrolled use of the plea has led to shockingly low sentences and insignificant fines which are not deterrent to crime. As a practical matter it accomplished little that is useful even where the Government has civil litigation pending. Moreover, a person permitted to plead nolo contendere admits his guilt for the purpose of imposing punishment for his acts and yet, for all other purposes, and as far as the public is concerned, persists in th is denial of wrongdoing. It is no wonder that the public regards consent to such a plea by the Government as an admission that it has only a technical case at most and that the whole proceeding was just a fiasco.

For these reasons, government attorneys have been instructed for many years not to consent to nolo pleas except in the most unusual circumstances, and to do so then only with Departmental approval. Federal prosecutors should oppose the acceptance of a nolo plea, unless the responsible Assistant Attorney General concludes that the circumstances are so unusual that acceptance of the plea would be in the public interest.

[updated September 2006] [cited in USAM 6-2.000; USAM 6-4.320; USAM 9-28.1300]

9-27.520
Offers to Plead Nolo Contendere—Offer of Proof

In any case in which a defendant seeks to enter a plea of nolo contendere, the attorney for the government should make an offer of proof of the facts known to the government to support the conclusion that the defendant has in fact committed the offense charged. See also USAM 9-16.010.

Comment. If a defendant seeks to avoid admitting guilt by offering to plead nolo contendere, the attorney for the government should make an offer of proof of the facts known to the government to support the conclusion that the defendant has in fact committed the offense charged. This should be done even in the rare case in which the government does not oppose the entry of a nolo plea. In addition, as is the case with respect to guilty pleas, the attorney for the government should urge the court to require the defendant to admit publicly the facts underlying the criminal charges. These precautions should minimize the effectiveness of any subsequent efforts by the defendant to portray himself/herself as technically liable perhaps, but not seriously culpable.

9-27.530
Argument in Opposition of Nolo Contendere Plea

If a plea of nolo contendere is offered over the government's objection, the attorney for the government should state for the record why acceptance of the plea would not be in the public interest; and should oppose the dismissal of any charges to which the defendant does not plead nolo contendere.

Comment. When a plea of nolo contendere is offered over the government's objection, the prosecutor should take full advantage of Rule 11(b), Federal Rules of Criminal Procedure, to state for the record why acceptance of the plea would not be in the public interest. In addition to reciting the facts that could be proved to show the defendant's guilt, the prosecutor should bring to the court's attention whatever arguments exist for rejecting the plea. At the very least, such a forceful presentation should make it clear to the public that the government is unwilling to condone the entry of a special plea that may help the defendant avoid legitimate consequences of his/her guilt. If the nolo plea is offered to fewer than all charges, the prosecutor should also oppose the dismissal of the remaining charges.

[cited in USAM 6-4.320]

9-27.600
Entering into Non-prosecution Agreements in Return for Cooperation—Generally

Except as hereafter provided, the attorney for the government may, with supervisory approval, enter into a non-prosecution agreement in exchange for a person's cooperation when, in his/her judgment, the person's timely cooperation appears to be necessary to the public interest and other means of obtaining the desired cooperation are unavailable or would not be effective.

Comment.

In many cases, it may be important to the success of an investigation or prosecution to obtain the testimonial or other cooperation of a person who is himself/herself implicated in the criminal conduct being investigated or prosecuted. However, because of his/her involvement, the person may refuse to cooperate on the basis of his/her Fifth Amendment privilege against compulsory self-incrimination. In this situation, there are several possible approaches the prosecutor can take to render the privilege inapplicable or to induce its waiver.

First, if time permits, the person may be charged, tried, and convicted before his/her cooperation is sought in the investigation or prosecution of others. Having already been convicted himself/herself, the person ordinarily will no longer have a valid privilege to refuse to testify and will have a strong incentive to reveal the truth in order to induce the sentencing judge to impose a lesser sentence than that which otherwise might be found appropriate.

Second, the person may be willing to cooperate if the charges or potential charge against him/her are reduced in number or degree in return for his/her cooperation and his/her entry of a guilty plea to the remaining charges. An agreement to file a motion pursuant to Sentencing Guideline 5K1.1 or Rule 35 of the Federal Rules of Criminal Procedure after the defendant gives full and complete cooperation is the preferred method for securing such cooperation. Usually such a concession by the government will be all that is necessary, or warranted, to secure the cooperation sought. Since it is certainly desirable as a matter of policy that an offender be required to incur at least some liability for his/her criminal conduct, government attorneys should attempt to secure this result in all appropriate cases, following the principles set forth in USAM 9-27.430 to the extent practicable.

The third method for securing the cooperation of a potential defendant is by means of a court order under 18 U.S.C. §§ 6001-6003. Those statutory provisions govern the conditions under which uncooperative witnesses may be compelled to testify or provide information notwithstanding their invocation of the privilege against compulsory self incrimination. In brief, under the so-called "use immunity" provisions of those statutes, the court may order the person to testify or provide other information, but neither his/her testimony nor the information he/she provides may be used against him/her, directly or indirectly, in any criminal case except a prosecution for perjury or other failure to comply with the order. Ordinarily, these "use immunity" provisions should be relied on in cases in which attorneys for the government need to obtain sworn testimony or the production of information before a grand jury or at trial, and in which there is reason to believe that the person will refuse to testify or provide the information on the basis of his/her privilege against compulsory self-incrimination. See USAM 9-23.000. Offers of immunity and immunity agreements should be in writing. Consideration should be given to documenting the evidence available prior to the immunity offer.

Finally, there may be cases in which it is impossible or impractical to employ the methods described above to secure the necessary information or other assistance, and in which the person is willing to cooperate only in return for an agreement that he/she will not be prosecuted at all for what he/she has done. The provisions set forth hereafter describe the conditions that should be met before such an agreement is made, as well as the procedures recommended for such cases.

It is important to note that these provisions apply only if the case involves an agreement with a person who might otherwise be prosecuted. If the person reasonably is viewed only as a potential witness rather than a potential defendant, and the person is willing to cooperate, there is no need to consult these provisions.

USAM 9-27.600 describes three circumstances that should exist before government attorneys enter into non-prosecution agreements in return for cooperation: the unavailability or ineffectiveness of other means of obtaining the desired cooperation; the apparent necessity of the cooperation to the public interest; and the approval of such a course of action by an appropriate supervisory official

Unavailability or Ineffectiveness of Other Means. As indicated above, non-prosecution agreements are only one of several methods by which the prosecutor can obtain the cooperation of a person whose criminal involvement makes him/her a potential subject of prosecution. Each of the other methods—seeking cooperation after trial and conviction, bargaining for cooperation as part of a plea agreement, and compelling cooperation under a "use immunity" order—involves prosecuting the person or at least leaving open the possibility of prosecuting him/her on the basis of independently obtained evidence. Since these outcomes are clearly preferable to permitting an offender to avoid any liability for his/her conduct, the possible use of an alternative to a non-prosecution agreement should be given serious consideration in the first instance.

Another reason for using an alternative to a non-prosecution agreement to obtain cooperation concerns the practical advantage in terms of the person's credibility if he/she testifies at trial. If the person already has been convicted, either after trial or upon a guilty plea, for participating in the events about which he/she testifies, his/her testimony is apt to be far more credible than if it appears to the trier of fact that he/she is getting off "scot free." Similarly, if his/her testimony is compelled by a court order, he/she cannot properly be portrayed by the defense as a person who has made a "deal" with the government and whose testimony is, therefore, suspect; his/her testimony will have been forced from him/her, not bargained for.

In some cases, however, there may be no effective means of obtaining the person's timely cooperation short of entering into a non-prosecution agreement. The person may be unwilling to cooperate fully in return for a reduction of charges, the delay involved in bringing him/her to trial might prejudice the investigation or prosecution in connection with which his/her cooperation is sought and it may be impossible or impractical to rely on the statutory provisions for compulsion of testimony or production of evidence. One example of the latter situation is a case in which the cooperation needed does not consist of testimony under oath or the production of information before a grand jury or at trial. Other examples are cases in which time is critical, or where use of the procedures of 18 U.S.C. § 6003 would unreasonably disrupt the presentation of evidence to the grand jury or the expeditious development of an investigation, or where compliance with the statute of limitations or the Speedy Trial Act precludes timely application for a court order.

Only when it appears that the person's timely cooperation cannot be obtained by other means, or cannot be obtained effectively, should the attorney for the government consider entering into a non-prosecution agreement.

Public Interest. If he/she concludes that a non-prosecution agreement would be the only effective method for obtaining cooperation, the attorney for the government should consider whether, balancing the cost of foregoing prosecution against the potential benefit of the person's cooperation, the cooperation sought appears necessary to the public interest. This "public interest" determination is one of the conditions precedent to an application under 18 U.S.C. § 6003 for a court order compelling testimony. Like a compulsion order, a non-prosecution agreement limits the government's ability to undertake a subsequent prosecution of the witness. Accordingly, the same "public interest" test should be applied in this situation as well. Some of the considerations that may be relevant to the application of this test are set forth in USAM 9-27.620.

Supervisory Approval. Finally, the prosecutor should secure supervisory approval before entering into a non-prosecution agreement. Prosecutors working under the direction of a United States Attorney must seek the approval of the United States Attorney or a supervisory Assistant United States Attorney. Departmental attorneys not supervised by a United States Attorney should obtain the approval of the appropriate Assistant Attorney General or his/her designee, and should notify the United States Attorney or Attorneys concerned. The requirement of approval by a superior is designed to provide review by an attorney experienced in such matters, and to ensure uniformity of policy and practice with respect to such agreements. This section should be read in conjunction with USAM 9-27.640, concerning particular types of cases in which an Assistant Attorney General or his/her designee must concur in or approve an agreement not to prosecute in ret urn for cooperation.

9-27.620
Entering into Non-prosecution Agreements in Return for Cooperation— Considerations to be Weighed

In determining whether, a person's cooperation may be necessary to the public interest, the attorney for the government, and those whose approval is necessary, should weigh all relevant considerations, including:

The importance of the investigation or prosecution to an effective program of law enforcement;

The value of the person's cooperation to the investigation or prosecution; and

The person's relative culpability in connection with the offense or offenses being investigated or prosecuted and his/her history with respect to criminal activity.

Comment. This paragraph is intended to assist Federal prosecutors, and those whose approval they must secure, in deciding whether a person's cooperation appears to be necessary to the public interest. The considerations listed here are not intended to be all-inclusive or to require a particular decision in a particular case. Rather they are meant to focus the decision-maker's attention on factors that probably will be controlling in the majority of cases.

Importance of Case. Since the primary function of a Federal prosecutor is to enforce the criminal law, he/she should not routinely or indiscriminately enter into non-prosecution agreements, which are, in essence, agreements not to enforce the law under particular conditions. Rather, he/she should reserve the use of such agreements for cases in which the cooperation sought concerns the commission of a serious offense or in which successful prosecution is otherwise important in achieving effective enforcement of the criminal laws. The relative importance or unimportance of the contemplated case is therefore a significant threshold consideration.

Value of Cooperation. An agreement not to prosecute in return for a person's cooperation binds the government to the extent that the person carries out his/her part of the bargain. See Santobello v. New York 404 U.S. 257 (1971); Wade v. United States, 112 S. Ct. 1840 (1992). Since such an agreement forecloses enforcement of the criminal law against a person who otherwise may be liable to prosecution, it should not be entered into without a clear understanding of the nature of the quid pro quo and a careful assessment of its probable value to the government. In order to be in a position adequately to assess the potential value of a person's cooperation, the prosecutor should insist on an "offer of proof" or its equivalent from the person or his/her attorney. The prosecutor can then weigh the offer in terms of the investigation or prosecution in connection with which cooperation is sought. In doing so, he/she should consider such questions as whether the cooperation will in fact be forthcoming, whether the testimony or other information provided will be credible, whether it can be corroborated by other evidence, whether it will materially assist the investigation or prosecution, and whether substantially the same benefit can be obtained from someone else without an agreement not to prosecute. After assessing all of these factors, together with any others that may be relevant, the prosecutor can judge the strength of his/her case with and without the person's cooperation, and determine whether it may be in the public interest to agree to forego prosecution under the circumstances.

Relative Culpability and Criminal History. In determining whether it may be necessary to the public interest to agree to forego prosecution of a person who may have violated the law in return for that person's cooperation, it is also important to consider the degree of his/her apparent culpability relative to others who are subjects of the investigation or prosecution as well as his/her history of criminal involvement. Of course, ordinarily it would not be in the public interest to forego prosecution of a high-ranking member of a criminal enterprise in exchange for his/her cooperation against one of his/her subordinates, nor would the public interest be served by bargaining away the opportunity to prosecute a person with a long history of serious criminal involvement in order to obtain the conviction of someone else on less serious charges. These are matters with regard to which the attorney for the government may find it helpful to consult with the investigating agenc y or with other prosecuting authorities who may have an interest in the person or his/her associates.

It is also important to consider whether the person has a background of cooperation with law enforcement officials, either as a witness or an informant, and whether he/she has previously been the subject of a compulsion order under 18 U.S.C. §§ 6001-6003 or has escaped prosecution by virtue of an agreement not to prosecute. The information regarding compulsion orders may be available by telephone from the Policy and Statutory Enforcement Unit in the Office of Enforcement Operations of the Criminal Division.

[updated October 2010]

9-27.630
Entering into Non-prosecution Agreements in Return for Cooperation—Limiting the Scope of Commitment

In entering into a non-prosecution agreement, the attorney for the government should, if practicable, explicitly limit the scope of the government's commitment to:

Non-prosecution based directly or indirectly on the testimony or other information provided; or

Non-prosecution within his/her district with respect to a pending charge, or to a specific offense then known to have been committed by the person.

Comment. The attorney for the government should exercise extreme caution to ensure that his/her non-prosecution agreement does not confer "blanket" immunity on the witness. To this end, he/she should, in the first instance, attempt to limit his/her agreement to non-prosecution based on the testimony or information provided. Such an "informal use immunity" agreement has two advantages over an agreement not to prosecute the person in connection with a particular transaction: first, it preserves the prosecutor's option to prosecute on the basis of independently obtained evidence if it later appears that the person's criminal involvement was more serious than it originally appeared to be; and second, it encourages the witness to be as forthright as possible since the more he/she reveals the more protection he/she will have against a future prosecution. To further encourage full disclosure by the witness, it should be made clear in the agreement that the government's forbearance from prosecution is conditioned upon the witness's testimony or production of information being complete and truthful, and that failure to testify truthfully may result in a perjury prosecution.

Even if it is not practicable to obtain the desired cooperation pursuant to an "informal use immunity" agreement, the attorney for the government should attempt to limit the scope of the agreement in terms of the testimony and transactions covered, bearing in mind the possible effect of his/her agreement on prosecutions in other districts.

It is important that non-prosecution agreements be drawn in terms that will not bind other Federal prosecutors or agencies without their consent. Thus, if practicable, the attorney for the government should explicitly limit the scope of his/her agreement to non-prosecution within his/her district. If

162

such a limitation is not practicable and it can reasonably be anticipated that the agreement may affect prosecution of the person in other districts, the attorney for the government contemplating such an agreement shall communicate the relevant facts to the Assistant Attorney General with supervisory responsibility for the subject matter. United States Attorneys may not make agreements which prejudice civil or tax liability without the express agreement of all affected Divisions and/or agencies. See also 9-16.000 et seq. for more information regarding plea agreements.

Finally, the attorney for the government should make it clear that his/her agreement relates only to non-prosecution and that he/she has no independent authority to promise that the witness will be admitted into the Department's Witness Security program or that the Marshal's Service will provide any benefits to the witness in exchange for his/her cooperation. This does not mean, of course, that the prosecutor should not cooperate in making arrangements with the Marshal's Service necessary for the protection of the witness in appropriate cases. The procedures to be followed in such cases are set forth in USAM 9-21.000.

9-27.640
Agreements Requiring Assistant Attorney General Approval

The attorney for the government should not enter into a non-prosecution agreement in exchange for a person's cooperation without first obtaining the approval of the Assistant Attorney General with supervisory responsibility over the subject matter, or his/her designee, when:

Prior consultation or approval would be required by a statute or by Departmental policy for a declination of prosecution or dismissal of a charge with regard to which the agreement is to be made; or

The person is:

A high-level Federal, state, or local official;

An official or agent of a Federal investigative or law enforcement agency; or

A person who otherwise is, or is likely to become of major public interest.

Comment. USAM 9-27.640 sets forth special cases that require approval of non-prosecution agreements by the responsible Assistant Attorney General or his/her designee. Subparagraph (1) covers cases in which existing statutory provisions and departmental policies require that, with respect to certain types of offenses, the Attorney General or an Assistant Attorney General be consulted or give his/her approval before prosecution is declined or charges are dismissed. For example, see USAM 6-4.245 (tax offenses); USAM 9-41.010 (bankruptcy frauds); USAM 9-90.020 (internal security offenses); (see USAM 9-2.400 for a complete listing of all prior approval and consultation requirements). An agreement not to prosecute resembles a declination of prosecution or the dismissal of a charge in that the end result in each case is similar: a person who has engaged in criminal activity is not prosecuted or is not prosecuted fully for his/her offense. Accordingly, attorneys for the government should obtain the approval of the appropriate Assistant Attorney General, or his/her designee, before agreeing not to prosecute in any case in which consultation or approval would be required for a declination of prosecution or dismissal of a charge.

Subparagraph (2) sets forth other situations in which the attorney for the government should obtain the approval of an Assistant Attorney General, or his/her designee, of a proposed agreement not to prosecute in exchange for cooperation. Generally speaking, the situations described will be cases of an exceptional or extremely sensitive nature, or cases involving individuals or matters of major public interest. In a case covered by this provision that appears to be of an especially sensitive nature, the Assistant Attorney General should, in turn, consider whether it would be appropriate to notify the Attorney General or the Deputy Attorney General.

9-27.641

Multi-District (Global) Agreement Requests

No district or division shall make any agreement, including any agreement not to prosecute, which purports to bind any other district(s) or division without the express written approval of the United States Attorney(s) in each affected district and/or the Assistant Attorney General of the Criminal Division.

The requesting district/division shall make known to each affected district/division the following information:

The specific crimes allegedly committed in the affected district(s) as disclosed by the defendant. (No agreement should be made as to any crime(s) not disclosed by the defendant.)

Identification of victims of crimes committed by the defendant in any affected district, insofar as possible.

The proposed agreement to be made with the defendant and the applicable Sentencing Guideline range.
See USAM 16.030 for a discussion of the requirement for consultation with investigative agencies and victims regarding pleas.

[cited in USAM 9-28.1000]

9-27.650

Records of Non-Prosecution Agreements

In a case in which a non-prosecution agreement is reached in return for a person's cooperation, the attorney for the government should ensure that the case file contains a memorandum or other written record setting forth the terms of the agreement. The memorandum or record should be signed or initialed by the person with whom the agreement is made or his/her attorney.

Comment. The provisions of this section are intended to serve two purposes. First, it is important to have a written record in the event that questions arise concerning the nature or scope of the agreement. Such questions are certain to arise during cross-examination of the witness, particularly if the existence of the agreement has been disclosed to defense counsel pursuant to the requirements of Brady v. Maryland, 373 U.S. 83 (1963) and Giglio v. United States, 405 U.S. 150 (1972). The exact terms of the agreement may also become relevant if the government attempts to prosecute the witness for some offense in the future. Second, such a record will facilitate identification by government attorneys (in the course of weighing future agreements not to prosecute, plea agreements, pre-trial diversion, and other discretionary actions) of persons whom the government has agreed not to prosecute.

The principal requirements of the written record are that it be sufficiently detailed that it leaves no doubt as to the obligations of the parties to the agreement, and that it be signed or initialed by the person with whom the agreement is made and his/her attorney, or at least by one of them.

9-27.710
Participation in Sentencing—Generally

During the sentencing phase of a Federal criminal case, the attorney for the government should assist the sentencing court by:

Attempting to ensure that the relevant facts are brought to the court's attention fully and accurately; and

Making sentencing recommendations in appropriate cases.

Comment. Sentencing in Federal criminal cases is primarily the function and responsibility of the court. This does not mean, however, that the prosecutor's responsibility in connection with a criminal case ceases upon the return of a guilty verdict or the entry of a guilty plea; to the contrary, the attorney for the government has a continuing obligation to assist the court in its determination of the sentence to be imposed. The prosecutor must be familiar with the guidelines generally and with the specific guideline provisions applicable to his or her case. In discharging these duties, the attorney for the government should, as provided in USAM 9-27.720 and 9-27.750, endeavor to ensure the accuracy and completeness of the information upon which the sentencing decisions will be based. In addition, as provided in USAM 9-27.730, in appropriate cases the prosecutor should offer recommendations with respect to the sentence to be imposed.

9-27.720
Establishing Factual Basis for Sentence

In order to ensure that the relevant facts are brought to the attention of the sentencing court fully and accurately, the attorney for the government should:

Cooperate with the Probation Service in its preparation of the presentence investigation report;

Review material in the presentence investigation report;

Make a factual presentation to the court when:

Sentence is imposed without a presentence investigation and report;

It is necessary to supplement or correct the presentence investigation report;

It is necessary in light of the defense presentation to the court; or

It is requested by the court; and

Be prepared to substantiate significant factual allegations disputed by the defense.

Comment.

Cooperation with Probation Service. To begin with, if sentence is to be imposed following a presentence investigation and report, the prosecutor should cooperate with the Probation Service in its preparation of the presentence report for the court. Under Rule 32(b), Federal Rules of Criminal Procedure, the report should contain information about the history and characteristics of the defendant, including any prior criminal record, financial condition, and any circumstances affecting the defendant's behavior that may be helpful in imposing sentence or in the correctional treatment of the defendant. While much of this information may be available to the Probation Service from sources other than the government, some of it may be obtainable only from prosecutorial or investigative files to which probation officers do not have access. For this reason, it is important that the attorney for the government respond promptly to Probation Service requests by providing the reque sted information whenever possible. The attorney for the government should also recognize the occasional desirability of volunteering information to the Probation Service especially in a district where the Probation Office is overburdened. Doing so may be the best way to ensure that important facts about the defendant come to its attention. In addition, the prosecutor should be particularly alert to the need to volunteer relevant information to the Probation Service in complex cases, since it cannot be expected that probation officers will obtain a full understanding of the facts of such cases simply by questioning the prosecutor or examining his/her files.

The relevant information can be communicated orally, or by making portions of the case file available to the probation officer, or by submitting a sentencing memorandum or other written presentation for inclusion in the presentence report. Whatever method he/she uses, however, the attorney for the government should bear in mind that since the report will be shown to the defendant and defense counsel, care should be taken to prevent disclosures that might be harmful to law enforcement interests.

Review of Presentence Report. Before the sentencing hearing, the prosecutor should always review the presentence report, which is prepared pursuant to Rule 32, Federal Rules of Criminal Procedure. Not only must the prosecutor be satisfied that the report is factually accurate, he or she must also pay attention to the initial determination of the base offense level. Further, the prosecutor must also consider all adjustments reflected in the report, as well as any recommendations for departure made by the probation office. These adjustments and potential departures can have a profound effect on the defendant's sentence. As advocates for the United States, prosecutors should be prepared to argue concerning those adjustments (and, if necessary, departures allowed by the guidelines) in order to arrive at a final result which adequately and accurately describes the defendant's conduct of offense, criminal history, and other factors related to sentencing.

Factual Presentation to Court. In addition to assisting the Probation Service with its presentence investigation, the attorney for the government may find it necessary in some cases to make a factual presentation directly to the court. Such a presentation is authorized by Rule 32(c), Federal Rules of Criminal Procedure, which requires the court to "afford counsel for the defendant and for the Government an opportunity to comment on the probation officer's determinations and on other matters relating to the appropriate sentence."

The need to address the court concerning the facts relevant to sentencing may arise in four situations: (a) when sentence is imposed without a presentence investigation and report; (b) when necessary to correct or supplement the presentence report; (c) when necessary in light of the defense presentation to the court; and (d) when requested by the court.

Furnishing Information in Absence of Presentence Report. Rule 32(b), Federal Rules of Criminal Procedure, authorizes the imposition of sentence without a presentence investigation and report, if the court finds that the record contains sufficient information to permit the meaningful exercise of sentencing authority under 18 U.S.C. § 3553. Imposition of sentence pursuant to this provision usually occurs when the defendant has been found guilty by the court after a non-jury trial, when the case is relatively simple and straightforward, when the defendant has taken the stand and has been cross-examined, and when it is the court's intention not to impose a prison sentence. In such cases, and any others in which sentence is to be imposed without benefit of a presentence investigation and report (such as when a report on the defendant has recently been prepared in connection with another case), it may be particularly important that the attorney for the government not take advantage of the opportunity afforded by *Rule 32(c), Federal Rules of Criminal Procedure*, to address the court, since there will be no later opportunity to correct or supplement the record. Moreover, even if government counsel is satisfied that all facts relevant to the sentencing decision are already before the court, he/she may wish to make a factual presentation for the record that makes clear the government's view of the defendant, the offense, or both.

Correcting or Supplementing Presentence Report. The attorney for the government should bring any significant inaccuracies or omissions to the Court's attention at the sentencing hearing, together with the correct or complete information.

Responding to Defense Assertions. Having read the presentence report before the sentencing hearing the defendant or his/her attorney may dispute specific factual statements made therein. More likely, without directly challenging the accuracy of the report, the defense presentation at the hearing may omit reference to the derogatory information in the report while stressing any favorable information and drawing all inferences beneficial to the defendant. Some degree of selectivity in the defense presentation is probably to be expected, and will be recognized by the court. There may be instances, however, in which the defense presentation, if not challenged, will leave the court with a view of the defendant or of the offense significantly different from that appearing in the presentence report. If this appears to be a possibility, the attorney for the government may respond by correcting factual errors in the defense presentation, pointing out facts and inferences, igno red by the defense, and generally reinforcing the objective view of the defendant and his/her offense as expressed in the presentence report.

Responding to Court's Requests. There may be occasions when the court will request specific information from government counsel at the sentencing hearing (as opposed to asking generally whether the government wishes to be heard). When this occurs, the attorney for the government should, of course, furnish the requested information if it is readily available and no prejudice to law enforcement interests is likely to result from its disclosure.

Substantiation of Disputed Facts. In addition to providing the court with relevant factual material at the sentencing hearing when necessary, the attorney for the government should be prepared to substantiate significant factual allegations disputed by the defense. This can be done by making the source of the information available for cross examination or if there is good cause for nondisclosure of his/her identity, by presenting the information as hearsay and providing other guarantees of its reliability, such as corroborating testimony by others. See United States v. Fatico, 579 F.2d 707, 713 (2d Cir. 1978).

9-27.730
Conditions for Making Sentencing Recommendations

The attorney for the government should make a recommendation with respect to the sentence to be imposed when:

The terms of a plea agreement so require it;

The public interest warrants an expression of the government's view concerning the appropriate sentence.

Comment. USAM 9-27.730 describes two situations in which an attorney for the government should make a recommendation with respect to the sentence to be imposed: when the terms of a plea agreement require it, and when the public interest warrants an expression of the government's view concerning the appropriate sentence. The phrase "make a recommendation with respect to the sentence to be imposed" is intended to cover tacit recommendations (i.e., agreeing to the defendant's request or not opposing the defendant's request) as well as explicit recommendations for a specific type of sentence (e.g., probation or a fine), for a specific condition of probation, a specific fine, or a specific term of imprisonment; and for concurrent or consecutive sentences.

The attorney for the government should be guided by the circumstances of the case and the wishes of the court concerning the manner and form in which sentencing recommendations are made. If the government's position with respect to the sentence to be imposed is related to a plea agreement with the defendant, that position must be made known to the court at the time the plea is entered. In other situations, the government's position might be conveyed to the probation officer, orally or in writing, during the presentence investigation; to the court in the form of a sentencing memorandum filed in advance of the sentencing hearing; or to the court orally at the time of the hearing.

Recommendations Required by Plea Agreement. ule 11(e)(1), Federal Rules of Criminal Procedure, authorizing plea negotiations, implicitly permits the prosecutor, pursuant to a plea agreement, to make a sentence recommendation, agree not to oppose the defendant's request for a specific sentence, or agree that a specific sentence is the appropriate disposition of the case. If the prosecutor has entered into a plea agreement calling for the government to take a certain position with respect to the sentence to be imposed, and the defendant has entered a guilty plea in accordance with the terms of the agreement, the prosecutor must perform his/her part of the bargain or risk having the plea invalidated. *Machibroda v. United States*, 368 U.S. 487, 493 (1962); *Santobello v. United States*, 404 U.S. 257, 262 (1971).

Recommendations Reflecting Defendant's Cooperation. Section 5K1.1 of the Sentencing Guidelines provides that, upon motion by the government, a court may depart below the guidelines to reflect a defendant's cooperation. Title 18 U.S.C. § 3553(e) permits the court to impose a sentence below an otherwise applicable statutory minimum sentence upon motion of the government based upon a defendant's cooperation in the investigation or prosecution of another. The Supreme Court held in Melendez v. United States, 116 S.Ct. 2057 (1996) that a district court may not reduce a sentence below the statutory mandatory minimum based on a motion pursuant to 5K1.1 unless the government specifically sought a reduction in the mandatory minimum. See also Fed. R. Crim. P. Rule 35(b).

Recommendations Warranted by the Public Interest. From time to time, unusual cases may arise in which the public interest warrants an expression of the government's view concerning the appropriate sentence, irrespective of the absence of a plea agreement. In some such cases, the court may invite or request a recommendation by the prosecutor, while in others the court may not wish to have a sentencing recommendation from the government. In either event, whether the public interest requires an expression of the government's view concerning the appropriate sentence in a particular case is a matter to be determined with care, preferably after consultation between the prosecutor handling the case and his/her supervisor—the United States Attorney or a Supervisory Assistant United States Attorney, or the responsible Assistant Attorney General or his/her designee.

The prosecutor should bear in mind the attitude of the court toward sentencing recommendations by the government, and should weigh the desirability of maintaining a clear separation of judicial and prosecutorial responsibilities against the likely consequences of making no recommendation. If the prosecutor has good reason to anticipate the imposition of a sanction that would be unfair to the defendant or inadequate in terms of society's needs, he/she may conclude that it would be in the public interest to attempt to avert such an outcome by offering a sentencing recommendation. For example, if the case is one in which the Sentencing Guidelines allow but do not require the imposition of a term of imprisonment, the imposition of a term of imprisonment plainly would be inappropriate, and the court has requested the government's view, the prosecutor should not hesitate to recommend or agree to the imposition of probation. On the other hand, if the responsible government attorney be lieves that a term of imprisonment is plainly warranted and that, under all the circumstances, the public interest would be served by making a recommendation to that effect, he/she should make such a recommendation even though the court has not invited it. Recognizing, however, that the primary responsibility for sentencing lies with the judiciary, government attorneys should avoid routinely taking positions with respect to sentencing, reserving their recommendations instead for those unusual cases in which the public interest warrants an expression of the government's view.

In connection with sentencing recommendations, the prosecutor should also bear in mind the potential value in some cases of the imposition of innovative conditions of probation if consistent with the Sentencing Guidelines. For example, in a case in which a sentencing recommendation would be appropriate and in which it can be anticipated that a term of probation will be imposed, the responsible government attorney may conclude that it would be appropriate to recommend, as a specific condition of probation, that the defendant participate in community service activities, or that he/she desist from engaging in a particular type of business.

9-27.740

Consideration to be Weighed in Determining Sentencing Recommendations

Consideration to be Weighed in Determining Sentencing

If the prosecutor makes a recommendation as to the sentence to be imposed within the applicable guideline range determined by the court, the prosecutor should consider the various purposes of sentencing, as noted below.

If the prosecutor makes a recommendation as to a sentence to be imposed after the court grants a motion for downward departure under Sentencing Guideline 5K1.1, the prosecutor should also consider the timeliness of the cooperation, the results of the cooperation, and the nature and extent of the cooperation when compared to other defendants in the same or similar cases in that district.

Comment. The Sentencing Reform Act was enacted to eliminate unwarranted disparity in sentencing. Both judicial discretion and the scope of prosecutorial recommendations have been limited, in those cases in which no departure is made from the applicable guideline range. The prosecutor, however, still has a significant role to play in making appropriate recommendations in cases involving either a sentence within the applicable range or a departure. In making a sentencing recommendation, the prosecutor should bear in mind that, by offering a recommendation, he/she shares with the court the responsibility for avoiding unwarranted sentence disparities among defendants with similar backgrounds who have been found guilty of similar conduct.

Applicable Sentencing Purposes. The attorney for the government should consider the seriousness of the defendant's conduct, and his/her background and personal circumstances, in light of the four purposes or objectives of the imposition of criminal sanctions:

To deter the defendant and others from committing crime;

To protect the public from further offenses by the defendant;
To assure just punishment for the defendant's conduct; and

To promote the correction and rehabilitation of the defendant.

The attorney for the government should recognize that not all of these objectives may be relevant in every case and that, for a particular offense committed by a particular offender, one of the purposes, or a combination of purposes, may be of overriding importance. For example, in the case of a young first offender who commits a minor, non-violent offense, the primary or sole purpose of sentencing might be rehabilitation. On the other hand, the primary purpose of sentencing a repeat violent offender might be to protect the public, and the perpetrator of a massive fraud might be sentenced primarily to deter others from engaging in similar conduct.

9-27.745
Unwarranted Sentencing Departures by the Court

If the court is considering a departure for a reason not allowed by the guidelines, the prosecutor should resist.

Comment. The prosecutor, with Departmental approval, may appeal a sentence which is unlawful or in violation of the Sentencing Guidelines. 18 U.S.C. § 3742(b). If such a sentence is imposed, the Appellate Section of the Criminal Division should be promptly notified so that an appeal can be considered.
9-27.750
Disclosing Factual Material to Defense

The attorney for the government should disclose to defense counsel, reasonably in advance of the sentencing hearing, any factual material not reflected in the presentence investigation report that he/she intends to bring to the attention of the court.

Comment. Due process requires that the sentence in a criminal case be based on accurate information. See, e.g., Moore v. United States, 571 F.2d 179, 182-84 (3d Cir. 1978). Accordingly, the defense should have access to all material relied upon by the sentencing judge, including memoranda from the prosecution (to the extent that considerations of informant safety permit), as well as sufficient time to review such material and an opportunity to present any refutation that can be mustered. See, e.g., United States v. Perri, 513 F.2d 572, 575 (9th Cir. 1975); United States v. Rosner, 485 F.2d 1213, 1229-30 (2d Cir. 1973), cert. denied, 417 U.S. 950 (1974); United States v. Robin, 545 F.2d 775 (2d Cir. 1976). USAM 9-27.750 is intended to facilitate satisfaction of these requirements by providing the defendant with notice of information not contained in the presentence report that the government plans to bring to the attention of the sentencing court.

9-27.760
Limitation on Identifying Uncharged Third-Parties Publicly
In all public filings and proceedings, federal prosecutors should remain sensitive to the privacy and reputation interests of uncharged third-parties. In the context of public plea and sentencing proceedings, this means that, in the absence of some significant justification, it is not appropriate to identify (either by name or unnecessarily-specific description), or cause a defendant to identify, a third-party wrongdoer unless that party has been officially charged with the misconduct at issue. In the unusual instance where identification of an uncharged third-party wrongdoer during a plea or sentencing hearing is justified, the express approval of the United States Attorney or his designee should be obtained prior to the hearing absent exigent circumstances. See USAM 9-16.500. In other less predictable contexts, federal prosecutors should strive to avoid unnecessary public references to wrongdoing by uncharged third-parties. With respect to bills of particulars that identify unindicted co-conspirators, prosecutors generally should seek leave to file such documents under seal. Prosecutors

shall comply, however, with any court order directing the public filing of a bill of particulars.

As a series of cases make clear, there is ordinarily "no legitimate governmental interest served" by the government's public allegation of wrongdoing by an uncharged party, and this is true "[r]egardless of what criminal charges may . . . b[e] contemplated by the Assistant United States Attorney against the [third-party] for the future." In re Smith, 656 F.2d 1101, 1106-07 (5th Cir. 1981). Courts have applied this reasoning to preclude the public identification of unindicted third-party wrongdoers in plea hearings, sentencing memoranda, and other government pleadings. See Finn v. Schiller, 72 F.3d 1182 (4th Cir. 1996); United States v. Briggs, 513 F.2d 794 (5th Cir. 1975); United States. v Anderson, 55 F.Supp.2d 1163 (D. Kan 1999); United States v. Smith, 992 F. Supp. 743 (D.N.J. 1998); see also USAM 9-11.130.

In all but the unusual case, any legitimate governmental interest in referring to uncharged third-party wrongdoers can be advanced through means other than those condemned in this line of cases. For example, in those cases where the offense to which a defendant is pleading guilty requires as an element that a third-party have a particular status (e.g., 18 U.S.C. § 203(a)(2)), the third-party can usually be referred to generically ("a Member of Congress"), rather than identified specifically ("Senator Jones"), at the defendant's plea hearing. Similarly, when the defendant engaged in joint criminal conduct with others, generic references ("another individual") to the uncharged third-party wrongdoers can be used when describing the factual basis for the defendant's guilty plea.

[new August 2002]

8-0

For matters involving taxes, collections, negotiations and plea agreements, see Appendix "B" for the complete Internal Revenue Service Policy.

Appendix "B"

MATTERS INVOLVING TAXES
AND
PLEA AGREEMENTS

IRS

Part 9. Criminal Investigation

Chapter 6. Trial and Court Related Activities

Section 2. Plea Agreements and Sentencing Process

9.6.2 Plea Agreements and Sentencing Process

- 9.6.2.1 Overview
- 9.6.2.2 Proposed Plea Agreement Situations
- 9.6.2.3 Concurrence or Non-concurrence of Special Agent in Charge Regarding Prosecution Reports
- 9.6.2.4 Restitution in Plea Agreements
- 9.6.2.5 Sentencing Process

9.6.2.1   **(07-21-2004)**

Overview

1. This section provides guidelines and procedures for processing referrals in proposed plea agreement situations. These procedures are designed to assist a taxpayer currently under investigation, who is represented by counsel, to negotiate a plea agreement.

2. The sentencing process follows after a defendant signs a plea agreement, enters a guilty plea, or is found guilty as the result of a trial.

3. The section also provides guidance to the special agent for communication with probation officers.

4. This section contains the following topics:

    A. Proposed Plea Agreement Situations

    B. Concurrence or Non-Concurrence of Special Agent in Charge Regarding Prosecution Reports

    C. The Sentencing Process

9.6.2.2   **(07-21-2004)**

Proposed Plea Agreement Situations

1. A taxpayer may enter into a plea agreement with the government at any stage of an investigation. Criminal Investigation (CI) does not have authority to initiate plea negotiations with the taxpayer because this authority rests solely with the Department of Justice (DOJ). A taxpayer must be represented by counsel to initiate plea discussions or negotiations.

Note:

If a taxpayer that is not represented by counsel expresses an interest in plea negotiation discussions, advise the taxpayer that in order to participate, he/she must be represented by counsel.

9.6.2.2.1   **(07-21-2004)**

Administrative Investigations

1. In an administrative investigation involving legal source income, when a taxpayer, through counsel, expresses a desire to participate in the expedited plea program, inform the taxpayer and his/her counsel that the willingness to enter into plea negotiations with DOJ in no way reduces the taxpayer's ultimate civil tax liability.

9.6.2.2.1.1   **(07-21-2004)**

Investigations Processed under the Expedited Plea Program Procedures (Tax Division Directive 111)

1. These investigations do not require the same degree of preparation as normal administrative tax investigations since they will not go to trial.

2. The investigations do require that sufficient evidence be obtained to constitute a referable matter that would meet the requirements of Federal Rules of Criminal Procedure Rule 11 (b)(3) (Fed. R. Crim. P. 11 (b)(3)) and the charges established by the investigation would adequately address the crime(s) committed by the taxpayer.

3. The IRS will take precautions to ensure that information furnished by the taxpayer, prior to formal plea discussions with DOJ, will not be prohibited from future use under the restrictions of Fed. R. Crim. P. 11(f) in the event that plea negotiations fail by reason of withdrawal or rejection by DOJ.

4. The expedited plea program procedure is designed to accommodate the interests of taxpayers who desire a speedy resolution of the investigation and prosecution, as well as the interest of the government in obtaining an appropriate resolution with the appropriate expenditure of investigative and prosecutorial resources.

5. Taxpayers requesting use of the expedited plea program procedure will be expected to cooperate with the IRS in the determination and satisfaction of their civil tax liabilities, as well as the criminal aspects. In the event the criminal investigation is completed by use of these procedures without establishing the appropriate civil deficiencies, the appropriate operating division of the IRS will complete the civil investigation.

6. For a plea agreement to be acceptable under the expedited plea program, it must:

    A. involve legal source income

    B. establish culpability for the violations charged

    C. include the most significant violation

    D. consider the totality of the fraud committed by the taxpayer

    E. not reduce tax return felony counts to misdemeanors

Note:

Investigations in which the taxpayer does not appear willing to enter an acceptable plea, or where the investigation has not established the general scope of the taxpayer's culpability, are inappropriate for inclusion in this program.

9.6.2.2.1.2   **(08-11-2008)**

Procedures Prior to Criminal Tax Counsel Pre-Referral Assistance

1. When a taxpayer, represented by counsel, expresses a desire to negotiate a plea agreement prior to the formal completion of an administrative investigation, the special agent will advise taxpayer's counsel of the following:

    A. Authority to engage in plea negotiations rests exclusively with DOJ.

    B. Counsel for the taxpayer must provide a written statement to CI confirming the taxpayer's desire to engage immediately in plea negotiations with DOJ. The IRS will make a referral to DOJ by forwarding the written proposal to enter a plea of guilty to the charges being investigated.

If approved by DOJ, Tax Division, it will be referred to the appropriate US Attorney's office for plea negotiations.

C. The taxpayer must be informed that he/she will be required to plead to the most significant violation involved, consistent with the Tax Division's Major Count Policy.

D. Plea negotiations have to be conducted by either the respective US Attorney's office or by DOJ, Tax Division.

E. The taxpayer must submit to an interview by the special agent and anything said or any information furnished can be used against the taxpayer in a criminal prosecution, as well as in any civil settlement.

F. The taxpayer must provide all records or information in his/her possession or to which the taxpayer has access, to the IRS for the years involved.

G. The charges being investigated and any proposal to enter into plea negotiations can be referred to DOJ, Tax Division only after CI is able to corroborate the elements of the offense being investigated or the admissions being made by the taxpayer (e.g., gross income in a §7203 investigation or documentation relating to an unreported material matter in a §7206 (1) investigation, etc.). Criminal Investigation must have sufficient evidence to constitute a referable matter to DOJ.

2. The investigating special agent should review all records in enough detail to ensure that there are no significant undiscovered issues or tax losses in the investigations that have not been taken into

account in assessing the merits of the referral to DOJ, Tax Division.

3. The special agent should secure and review the taxpayer's returns for all years subsequent to the years under investigation and any open prior years to address any issues raised by those returns in assessing the merits of the referral.

4. The special agent should inquire and obtain the details, if appropriate, as to any other (open or closed) Federal, state, or local investigations relating to the taxpayer.

9.6.2.2.1.3   **(08-11-2008)**

Pre-Referral Assistance From Criminal Tax Counsel

1. If CI determines that a referral for plea negotiations would be in the best interests of the government, Criminal Tax (CT) Counsel will be contacted for pre-referral assistance on the issues of whether:

    A. The presently available evidence is sufficient to meet the requirements of Fed. R. Crim P. 11(b)(3), specifically that a factual basis exists to support the plea of guilty to each of the counts considered for referral.

    B. The charges established by the investigation adequately address the crime(s) committed by the taxpayer.

2. At the option of the Special Agent in Charge (SAC), if CT Counsel concurs with CI that a referral should be made, CT Counsel will contact the taxpayer's counsel orally or in writing to accomplish the following:

    A. Confirm that the taxpayer wants to enter into plea negotiations with DOJ.

    B. Remind the taxpayer and his/her counsel of the charges being investigated and that the government will only consider a plea that adequately addresses those specific charges, i.e., the government will generally be looking for a plea of guilty to one or more of the specified charges.

    C. Confirm that the taxpayer is willing to be interviewed by the special agent and that the taxpayer will submit all records or information in his/her possession or to which he/she has access to the IRS for the tax years involved.

3. If the taxpayer's counsel wants to proceed with negotiations, the SAC or CT Counsel will request the taxpayer's counsel provide a written statement that confirms the taxpayer's wish to immediately engage in plea negotiations with the US Attorney or DOJ, Tax Division.

9.6.2.2.2   **(07-21-2004)**

Grand Jury Investigations

1. The US Attorney's office or DOJ will be responsible for negotiating any plea agreement during a grand jury investigation. If a plea involves tax violations, authorization must be obtained from DOJ, Tax Division.

2. The taxpayer and his/her counsel will be informed that the willingness to enter into plea negotiations with DOJ in no way reduces the taxpayer's ultimate civil tax liability.

3. The taxpayer must be informed that he/she will be required to plead to the most significant violation involved, consistent with the Tax Division's Major Count Policy.

9.6.2.2.3 (08-11-2008)

Prosecution Recommendation Report

1. After the written statement is provided and is deemed legally sufficient by CT Counsel, the special agent will forward a modified prosecution recommendation report containing the following information:

   A. The title page of the prosecution recommendation report will state that this matter involves a proposed plea agreement, and is a limited referral to DOJ only for purposes of negotiation, and if possible, finalizing a plea.

   B. The taxpayer's identification, personal history, and a history of business or income-producing activities.

   C. The nature of the taxpayer's fraudulent activity and the evidence, including available exhibits, to support acceptance of a plea to the charges under investigation.

   D. Any indication of non-tax crimes (Federal, state, or local) for which the taxpayer may be or has been under investigation.

   E. A recommendation for prosecution.

   F. Documentation that the taxpayer and/or the representative have provided all available records for all years involved in the investigation so it is clear there are no significant undiscovered issues in the investigation which have not been taken into account in assessing the merits of the investigation. This documentation should include all relevant conduct, which is necessary for presentation to the court for sentencing purposes.

G. A description of the nature and extent of the records supplied and the specific conclusions reached by the special agent and/or revenue agent who reviewed them.

H. Documentation of interview(s) with the taxpayer that reflect a thorough review of the issues in the investigation. (The taxpayer must submit to interview(s)).

I. A complete and thorough discussion of the nature and extent of the taxpayer's cooperation.

J. A summary and evaluation of the taxpayer's returns for all years under investigation, and subsequent to the years under investigation, addressing any issues raised by those returns in assessing the merits of the investigation. This summary will, where practical, include a computation reflecting the tax ramifications of the taxpayers' actions.

K. A discussion as to the potential range of sentences the taxpayer may receive based on the evidence available for use under the Sentencing Guidelines.

2. Criminal Tax Counsel will review the prosecution recommendation report for legal sufficiency pursuant to these guidelines. Criminal Tax Counsel will prepare a Criminal Evaluation Memo (CEM) for the SAC, which reflects CT Counsel's evaluation of the merits of the criminal prosecution. Contained within the CEM will be a section noting CT Counsel's concurrence or nonconcurrence with the prosecution recommendation.

3. If it is determined that prosecution is warranted, the SAC will refer the investigation to DOJ, Tax Division, recommending prosecution

and the initiation of plea negotiations in accordance with the written request of taxpayer's counsel.

A. A copy of the prosecution recommendation report with exhibits will be forwarded to Assistant Attorney General, Tax Division, Criminal Section, DOJ, 950 Pennsylvania Avenue, NW, Room 4744, Washington, DC 20530–0001, Attn: Chief, (Southern, Northern, or Western) Enforcement Section. (Send to the attention of the appropriate Enforcement Section Chief).

B. The SAC will telephone the DOJ liaison attorney to state that such a report is being submitted to their office. The DOJ attorney will contact the SAC by telephone to acknowledge receipt of the report.

4. The DOJ, Tax Division has 30 days after receipt of the referral from the SAC to either authorize prosecution consistent with the proposed plea bargain, or disapprove the negotiation of such a plea.

A. If DOJ, Tax Division objects to proceeding with the plea discussions, or the evidence submitted is insufficient to meet the requirements of Tax Division Directive III, and Fed. R. Crim. P. 11(f), DOJ, the Tax Division will immediately notify the SAC. For administrative investigations, DOJ, Tax Division will then notify the taxpayer's counsel in writing that the investigation is being returned to the IRS and all exhibits and files will be returned to the IRS.

B. If DOJ, Tax Division authorizes prosecution, it will refer all documents to the appropriate US Attorney's Office, who may then undertake plea negotiations with the taxpayer and his/her counsel. The US Attorney's Office may accept a plea to the specified major count without further authorization from DOJ, Tax Division. If the US Attorney's office desires to accept a plea to any count other than the specified major count, the approval of DOJ, Tax Division is required.

5. No information or evidence submitted to the US Attorney by the taxpayer or counsel during the course of plea negotiations will be forwarded to the IRS unless they expressly authorize the IRS' use of such information. In these situations, a written waiver of the Rule 11(f) restrictions should be obtained.

6. Upon return of an investigation, the IRS, after considering all relevant facts, will determine whether to continue with the investigation.

9.6.2.2.4   **(08-11-2008)**

Pleas Involving Title 18 Seizures and Forfeitures

1. The plea agreement must include a violation of one of the following offenses charged in the indictment or criminal information to ensure forfeitability of the property:

   A. 18 USC §1956

   B. 18 USC §1957

   C. 18 USC §1960

   D. 31 USC §5317(c)(2)

   E. 31 USC §5313(a)

    F.   31 USC §5324(a)

2. Additional requirements in plea agreements are contained in the Department of Treasury Executive Office of Asset Forfeiture (TEOAF) Directive 17.

9.6.2.3   **(08-11-2008)**

Concurrence or Non-concurrence of Special Agent in Charge Regarding Prosecution Reports

1. The SAC will approve the prosecution recommendation report and make the appropriate referral.

2. If the SAC does not approve the recommendation of the special agent, the SAC will prepare a memorandum documenting or explaining the reason(s) for not approving the prosecution recommendation report. The memorandum and prosecution recommendation report will be returned to the originating Supervisory Special Agent (SSA).

3. For sensitive investigations (those involving any of the following: a currently serving elected Federal official, a currently serving Article III judge; a currently serving high-level Executive Branch official; a currently serving elected statewide official; a currently serving member of the highest court of the state; a mayor currently serving a population of 250,000 or more; perjury in the US Tax Court; and an exempt organization), the SAC will forward the prosecution recommendation report to the Director, Field Operations with a brief cover memorandum asking for the concurrence of the Director, Field Operations. The investigation may not be referred until the written concurrence of the Director, Field Operations is obtained. See IRM 9.4.1, General, Primary and

Subject Investigations, subsection 9.4.1.6.3 for sensitive investigations.

9.6.2.4 (08-11-2008)

Restitution in Plea Agreements

1. Restitution is often ordered in criminal tax cases pursuant to a plea agreement, and may also be required as condition of probation. Including restitution as part of the plea agreement is an effective method for the Assistant United States Attorney to facilitate civil resolution of a criminal case and the inclusion of the taxpayer's cooperation in the civil settlement as part of the plea agreement. See LEM 9.14.2 for court ordered restitution for refund crimes.

9.6.2.5 (08-11-2008)

Sentencing Process

1. The ultimate goal of every criminal prosecution is not merely obtaining a conviction, but obtaining a sentence sufficient to discourage similar criminal violations by other taxpayers. Therefore, the special agent should devote the same attention and energy to the sentencing process as to the investigation and trial processes.

9.6.2.5.1 (08-11-2008)

Communication with Probation Officers

1. Whenever a conviction is obtained, the special agent should contact the US Probation Officer assigned to prepare the pre-sentence report, and furnish a copy of the prosecution recommendation report and any other information which may speak to relevant conduct in setting forth the full magnitude of the defendant's conduct.

2. Information to be furnished to the probation officer should include, but is not limited to the following:

   A. An account of the harm caused to the government or other victims.

   B. An explanation of the applicability of any sentencing factors listed in the Federal Sentencing Guidelines Manual.

   C. Any indications of any relevant conduct which might be useful to the probation officer in preparing the pre-sentence report and sentencing recommendation.

Note:

Relevant conduct includes conduct of the defendant that is outside the offense of conviction, but is part of the same or similar pattern of conduct as the count(s) of conviction. The US Sentencing Guidelines allow for consideration of uncharged conduct in calculating the appropriate sentencing range. The standard of proof necessary to utilize relevant conduct for sentencing purposes is a preponderance of the evidence.

3. Upon conviction, the prosecution recommendation report may be disclosed to a probation officer for the purpose of preparing the report contemplated by Fed. R. Crim. P. 32(c). The disclosure of the prosecution recommendation report to probation officers is authorized by 26 USC §6103(h)(4). However, information contained in the report shall not be disclosed if such disclosure would identify a confidential informant or seriously impair a civil or criminal tax investigation.

4. Occasionally, probation officers will request tax information from the IRS as part of a pre-sentence investigation in a non-tax

criminal matter. Disclosures may be made to probation officers in these circumstances only as provided in 26 USC §6103(c). Treasury Regulation §301.6103(c)1 provides the format that must be followed in any taxpayer authorization or waiver that is submitted for the purpose of allowing a probation officer to receive tax information.

5. The special agent must emphasize, to both the probation officer and the Assistant US Attorney, the importance that CI attaches to the sentence imposed, and the importance of including restitution. It is vital to point out the effect that the sentence and restitution may have on IRS compliance efforts among similarly situated individuals.

6. Following a conviction for criminal tax violations, courts in some instances specify the sentence imposed is conditioned upon satisfactory settlement and/or payment of civil liability for taxes and penalties, and the satisfactory payment of restitution. See IRM 9.5.14 concerning the conditions of probation in civil tax matters.

7. The SAC will take whatever steps are necessary to initiate appropriate legal action in any instance where the taxpayer has failed to comply with the conditions of the sentence. Title 26 USC §6103(h)(4) permits the disclosure of information contained in taxpayer delinquent account files to a US Probation Officer in a judicial proceeding pertaining to tax administration for the purpose of informing the court of any non-compliance with the terms of the taxpayer's sentence.

9.6.2.5.2

Costs of Prosecution

1. Title 26 explicitly provides that, in addition to incarceration and fines, defendants convicted of tax offenses "shall" pay "costs of prosecution" . The costs that defendants are required to pay are limited to those set out in Title 28 USC §1920. See IRM 9.6.4 concerning recoverable costs of prosecution for additional information.

Epilog

The federal justice system is a complex arena for even the experienced professional. This book, is designed to let the "average" person understand the complexities of plea negotiations, entering a plea agreement and the unexpected surprises at sentencing.

The "Beast", known as "relevant conduct", lurks in every Agreement. For example, if a defendant faces one hundred counts in an Indictment and pleads guilty to "just" two, which may give him or her a sense of relief, at sentencing, that defendant will be held accountable for ALL of the counts in that Indictment. In other words, if a defendant is indicted for five ounces of crack cocaine, but pursuant to a Plea Agreement they plead guilty to four grams, at sentencing, the defendant will be held accountable for the five ounces and facing a mandatory minimum of five years in a federal prison.

If a defendant goes to trial and is acquitted of counts in an Indictment, at sentencing on the count or counts for which they were convicted, they will face sentencing on the acquitted conduct, under the auspices of the "relevant conduct" monster.

Be very careful in navigating the federal waters, or the Devil will get your soul.

Daniel

About the Author

2011

Daniel Storm

Mr. Storm is Native American and ascribes to the Blackfoot heritage and ways. He grew up in Illinois and Wisconsin, where he attended the University of Wisconsin and ultimately studied law. After college, he participated in defending some of America's most notable crime figures, while associated with prestigious law firms.

As an author of numerous crime/fiction novels, he spends hours creating stories that compel readers to devote their undivided attention. Internationally, he is on the threshold of tremendous success, despite his retaining control of his stories, the production of his books and distribution.

He lives near Milwaukee with his German Shepherd, Merlin. He enjoys seeing the sites in Wisconsin on his Harley.

As a Viet Nam veteran, Storm works within the Wisconsin community to assist soldiers and military families, both of those in active service, and veterans and their families.

www.danielstormauthor.com

Another Necessity Book!